Surviving Disclosure

A Partner's Guide for Healing the Betrayal of Intimate Trust

by

JENNIFER P. SCHNEIDER M.D., PH.D.

AND M. DEBORAH CORLEY, PH.D.

THIS BOOK IS A COMPANION TO *DISCLOSING SECRETS: AN ADDICT'S GUIDE FOR WHEN, TO WHOM, AND HOW MUCH TO REVEAL*

FOR INFORMATION CONTACT:
Jennifer P. Schneider M.D., Ph.D.
3052 N Palomino Park Loop
Tucson, AZ 85712
(520) 990-7886

M. Deborah Corley, Ph.D.
Sante Center for Healing
914 Country Club Road
Argyle, TX 76226
(800) 258-4250

Please visit our websites at:
www.jenniferschneider.com
www.santecenter.com

ALL RIGHTS RESERVED

No portion of this publication may be reproduced, stored in any electronic system, or transmitted in any form or by any means, electronic, mechanical photocopy, recording or otherwise, without written permission from the authors. Brief quotations may be used in literary reviews.

Authors' note:

The quotations in this book come from real people but have been edited for clarity and changed to protect the individuals' confidentiality. Some stories and circumstances portrayed in these pages are composite in nature, combined to form illustrative viewpoints, characters and stories. Any resemblance of such composites to any actual persons is entirely coincidental.

Copyright © 2012 Jennifer P. Schneider M.D. Ph.D. and
M. Deborah Corley Ph,.D.

ISBN: 1477608303

ISBN 13: 9781477608302

Library of Congress Control Number: 2012910397

CreateSpace, North Charleston, SC

Advance Acclaim for *Surviving Disclosure: A Partner's Guide for Healing the Betrayal of Intimate Trust*

"In *Surviving Disclosure* Drs. Schneider and Corley offer a compassionate and thorough guide to help wade through the murky waters of pain and confusion following the disclosure of sexual secrets. Their clinical experience sensitively offers help to partners sorting through the many decisions and difficulties that are faced with the betrayal of trust. This book is sure to become a critical companion for those on the path toward healing as well as for the clinicians who treat them."

Kenneth M. Adams, Ph.D., CSAT, Author of *Silently Seduced: When Parents Make Their Children Partners* and *When He's Married to Mom: How to Help Mother-Enmeshed Men Open Their Hearts to True Love and Commitment* and Clinical Director of Kenneth M. Adams and Assoc.

"As professionals steadily refine the process of addiction recovery, there remains far too little focus on the profound betrayal experienced by those close to addicts-whose love and relationship trust has been broken. This book is a refreshingly validating, balanced and useful healing guide for those whose belief in trust, love and commitment have been disrupted by being in relationship to an addict. There is hope and healing in these pages!"

Robert Weiss LCSW, CSAT-S Author, Educator: Sex & Intimacy Disorders Expert Elements Behavioral Health

"Partners of addicts are often traumatized when they learn of the secret life of the addict. Through this incredible resource, Schneider and Corley share with partners what to expect and how to support themselves through this very difficult process. This is an essential guide for any partner experiencing disclosure".

Stefanie Carnes, PhD, LMFT Author of *Mending a Shattered Heart a Guide for Partners of Sex Addicts* and *Facing Heartbreak: Steps to Recovery for Partners of Sex Addicts*.

"Jennifer Schneider and Deb Corley, both towering leaders in the field of sex addiction recovery, have updated and improved their already classic book about disclosing secrets by turning it into two companion texts, one specifically written for the partner, *Surviving Disclosure*. The chapter on disclosing to children is especially useful in meeting the needs of this vulnerable population. The inclusion of a set of frequently asked questions is especially useful for those seeking the best way to take one of the hardest and most important steps toward healing damaged relationships. There is no better way to approach the disclosure of secrets than this book and its companion for addicts. Together they will help guide many relationships to a healthier life."

Bill Herring, MA,
Private Practice, Atlanta, GA.

"For partners of sex addicts, disclosure is the pivotal event in moving forward with life and the relationship. While disclosure brings both hope and fear, Drs. Schneider and Corley combine their expertise to show partners how to survive and heal. Partners will find wisdom, direction and hope in this book."

Milton S. Magness, D Min, MA Psy, CSAT, Author of *Thirty Days to Hope & Freedom From Sexual Addiction, Hope & Freedom for Sexual Addicts and Their Partners,* and *I Can Stop DVD series.*

"Jennifer Schneider and Deb Corley leave no stone unturned in providing the necessary information to help partners of addicts cope with lies and betrayals through addiction. In an area that is dark and feels hopeless, *Surviving Disclosure* shines a light and helps couples find their way back to each other. This guide matches no other in terms of its inclusiveness of all the ins and outs of what is experienced through the process of disclosure."

Joe Kort, Ph.D., Founder of The Center for Relationship and Sexual Health

"Jennifer Schneider and Deborah Corley have pioneered in the rollercoaster world of disclosure and brought real help to both addicts and partners. This new version will be appreciated by all involved. A must read for recovering people and their therapists."

Patrick Carnes, Ph.D. Leading author and researcher in the field of sex addiction

"*Disclosing Secrets* and *Surviving Disclosure* are comprehensive guides for addicts and their families to do what is most frightening - become honest and transparent to the ones they love. In easy and clear language Schneider and Corley take people step-by-step through the process. Partners and other family members ask, How much do I want to know, how can I stay, is this really everything, and how can I ever forgive? For therapists, these books are invaluable tools to help recovering addicts and their families heal from the destruction of addiction. Thank you Jennifer and Deb for making that process easier and less scary for everyone involved, including clinicians!"

Ann Foster, Founder & President, Millennium Counseling Center

"Disclosure is one of the most difficult tasks for the addict and can be the most traumatizing for the partner. The authors provide a solid framework to help the partner understand the reasons for the disclosure and what some of the pitfalls are, if not done properly. This is a must read for all partners and certainly for all therapists working in this area. This book should be given to every partner when they enter therapy, before disclosure. An excellent resource."

Barbara Levinson Ph.D, RN, LMFT, LSOTP, Certified Sex Therapist Diplomate, The Center for Healthy Sexuality, Houston, TX

"Groundbreaking work and extremely important to those confronting disclosure in their relationship. A thoughtful, and thorough guide and by far the best on the market! This invaluable book will help avoid pitfalls in the disclosure process and shape a positive and informed outcome for those impacted by sex addiction."

Cara W. Tripodi, LCSW, CSAT-S, Executive Director, STAR/Sexual Trauma & Recovery, Inc.

"Dr. Schneider and Dr. Corley adeptly describe the pain of living with sexual betrayal and the ensuing trauma that comes with chronic deception. In *Surviving Disclosure*, a person climbing out of disclosure despair will find answers, relief, and hope. For clinicians assisting the brave folks recovering their sexual lives, this is an essential text for the office library and bibliotherapy."

Kelly McDaniel LPC, NCC, CSAT Private practice San Antonio, TX
Author of *Ready to Heal: Breaking Free of Addictive Relationships*. Contributing author of *Making Advances: A Comprehensive Guide to Treating Women Addicted to Sex and Love*.

"*Surviving Disclosure* is a timely and immensely useful guidebook for helping partners survive the emotionally difficult disclosure process, using compassionate, yet direct intervention. Especially useful are the self-reflection exercises, and thoughtful suggestions about how and what to tell children. I recommend all therapists working with couples facing the disclosure of sexual betrayal to read and use this fine resource. The FAQ section is tremendous!

Anna Valenti-Anderson, LCSW, LISAC,
CSAT Private Practice, Phoenix, AZ

"Drs. Schneider and Corley have done it again! They've succeeded in providing two masterfully written, practical and invaluable manuals for those struggling with disclosure. Their newly released addict's guide and the accompanying guide for partners surviving disclosure, offer essential step-by-step guidance for a variety of disclosure circumstances, current research, and "how-to" resources to move beyond the pain and trauma of discovery. These guides are an invaluable "***must read***" for individuals who are struggling with the distress of sex addiction, disclosure and for professionals who work with couples and sexual infidelity."

Debra L. Kaplan, MA, LAC, LISAC, CSAT-S,
Private Practice, Tucson, AZ

"Integrity and vulnerability are the heart of all healthy relationships. Schneider and Corley lead the way, assisting couples in developing the courage to embrace these foundational practices, and providing them with a map for the journey. Their work is timely and essential!"

Sonnee D. Weedn, Ph.D., Clinical and Forensic Psychologist
Founder of Sonnee Weedn Institute for Integrative Therapy.

"In the area of guiding partners of sex addicts through the rocky waters of disclosure Corley & Schneider's *Surviving Disclosure* is a beacon of light illuminating the way for women and men to reclaim their lives and restore trust in their relationships after the ravages of sex addiction."

Alexandra Katehakis, MA, author of "Erotic Intelligence: Igniting Hot Healthy Sex While in Recovery from Sex Addiction"

About the Authors

Jennifer P. Schneider, M.D., Ph.D received her B.S. from Cornell University, her M.S. and Ph.D. in Human Genetics from the University of Michigan, and her M.D. from the University of Arizona College of Medicine. She is Board Certified in Internal Medicine, certified by the American Society of Addiction Medicine, and is a Diplomate of the American Academy of Pain Management. After practicing Internal Medicine for many years, she then specialized in treating patients who were living with chronic pain. In addition, for over 25 years she has been a researcher, speaker, and author in the field of compulsive sexual disorders, with a special interest in the effect of sex addiction on the family. Dr. Schneider has been Associate Editor of the journal *Sexual Addiction & Compulsivity* for many years, and has authored many articles, book chapters, and several books in the field. In 1998 she won the Patrick Carnes Award for lifetime contribution to the sex addiction field and in 2007 the Society for the Advancment of Sexual Health (SASH) Award for lifetime contributions to research in the sex addiction field.

M. Deborah Corley, Ph.D. received her B.A. from the University of Colorado at Colorado Springs and her M.A. and Ph.D. from Texas Woman's University. She is co-founder and co-owner of Santé Center for Healing, a residential treatment center for addictions near Denton, Texas. She serves as clinical consultant to the Santé treatment team and faculty for the courses Santé co-sponsors for professionals with the UT Southwestern Medical School. She won the 2008 Merit Award from Society for the Advancement of Sexual Health (SASH), the 1999 Carnes Award for outstanding achievement in the field of sex addiction and was the co-recipient with Dr. Schneider of the Clinician's Most Valuable Article Award by the American Foundation for Addiction Research in 2003 for their work on disclosure. She is the past president of the Board for SASH and a clinical member of the American Association of Marriage and Family Therapists. Licensed both as an addiction treatment specialist and marriage and family therapist, Deb has over 25 years of experience working with and conducting research on addictive disorders and high risk families. As an international speaker in the US and Canada, her focus on treatment of addictions, trauma resolution, disclosure, interpersonal neurobiology and meeting attachment needs is well received.

Other Books by the Authors

By Jennifer P Schneider:

The Myth of the Jewish Race, with Raphael Patai, 1976.

Back From Betrayal: Recovering from his Affairs, Third Edition, 2005.

Sex, Lies, and Forgiveness: Couples Speak on Healing From Sex Addiction, with Burt Schneider, Third Edition, 2004.

The Wounded Healer: Addiction-sensitive Approach to the Sexually Exploitative Professional, with Richard Irons, 1999.

Embracing Recovery from Chemical Dependence, with M. Deborah Corley and Richard Irons, 2003.

Disclosing Secrets: When, to Whom, and How Much to Reveal, with M. Deborah Corley, 2002.

Untangling the Web: Breaking Free from Sex, Porn, and Fantasy Addiction in the Internet Age, with Robert Weiss, 2006.

Living with Chronic Pain, Second Edition, 2009.

By M. Deborah Corley:

Making Advances: A Comprehensive Guide to Treatment of Female Sex and Love Addicts, edited by Marnie Ferree, 2012.

Embracing Recovery from Chemical Dependence, with Jennifer P. Schneider and Richard Irons, 2003.

Disclosing Secrets: When, to Whom, and How Much to Reveal, with Jennifer P. Schneider, 2002.

Acknowledgments

We would like to thank all the addicts and partners who have participated in our research over the years, as well as those clients who have given permission to use their original work. We too would like to thank Bill Herring for his input on our surveys for the Disclosure of Relapse research, Joshua Hook, PhD from University of North Texas for help in analysis of the data, David Delmonico, Ph.D. from Duquesne University for seuring IRB approval for human subject research, and Robert Kafes and Debra Kaplan for their review of the FAQ. Special thanks go to Marni Dittmar, librarian at Tucson Medical Center Medical Library, for facilitating library research in the field.

To our daughters

Contents

Acknowledgments ix
Preface xv
Introduction 1

Chapter One: The Power of Disclosure: Why Addicts Disclose and why Partners Need Disclosure 5
Why Addicts Disclose 6
Why Partners Need Disclosure 7
Honesty – Not Just for Addicts 11
References 13

Chapter Two: Secrets and Lies: Lies Influence Relationships and Relationships Influence Lies 15
Several Types of Secrets 17
   The Emotional Secret 17
   The Secret That Isn't a Secret – The Elephant in the Living Room 20
Partners' Lies 21
   He Would Never Lie to Me 21
   Maybe He Lied to Other [Women] People, but He Wouldn't Lie to Me . 22
   Yes, He Lies, but He Loves me and That's All That Matters 22
   Yes, He Lies, but He's a Victim of Circumstances 23
   Yes, He Lies, but I Can Fix Him 23
   Yes, He Lies, but It's My Fault 23
References 24

Chapter Three: Is Disclosure Right for You? If, When, and How Much To Ask the Addict 25
Forgiveness 26
When to Tell 29
How Much to Tell 35

    Reveal Now, or Save the Worst for Later:
       The Pain of Staggered Disclosure..37
    Should I Ask For "All the Gory Details"......................................42
    Private Information vs. Secret Information................................43
  Interim Disclosures..44
  The Therapist and Secret-Keeping...45
  References...46

Chapter Four: Consequences of Disclosure 49
  Preparing to Manage Emotions..52
  Positive Outcomes of Disclosure..53
  Adverse Consequences of Disclosure for the Partner 56
    Adverse consequences for the Addict...61
  Do Partners Leave As A Result of Disclosure? 63
    Threats Before and After Disclosure...65
  Partners' Reactions to Disclosure of Relapse 66
  Conclusions..67
  References...68

Chapter Five: The Formal Disclosure: How to Do It Right 69
  How and What to Tell...74
  What to Expect If Your Mate Goes Into Addiction Treatment 77
  Steps to Preparing to Hear a Disclosure..78
  The Timing and Extent of Formal Disclosure..............................80
  Disclosure of Relapse 81
  References...81

Chapter Six: What to Tell the Kids...83
  Effects of Parental Addiction on the Children 84
  How, What and How Much Do We Tell.......................................89
  Children's Reactions to Disclosure (Parents' description) 92
  Timing of Disclosure to Children 94
  What Kids Want to Know..95
  How to Help Your Child Do Well... 102

Basic Repair Work 106
Other Ongoing Repair Work 107
References 109

Chapter Seven: The Other Disclosures 111
Learning About Your Mate's Relapse 114
He or She Exposed Me to a Health Risk. What Now? 118
When Long-Ago Secrets Have Not Been Revealed 119
When a Parent is Not the Biological Parent 120
When the Secret Involves a Neighbor or Friend 121
When You Learn that a Friend's Spouse is Having an Affair, Using Drugs, or Gambling Compulsively 122
When Your Mate has Disclosed to You that he is Gay or she is Lesbian 123
When You or Your Spouse Really Wants to Leave 124
References 126

Chapter Eight: Special Issues 127
Family Members 127
A New Love Relationship: When Your Partner is an Addict 132
Friends 135
Disclose After An Arrest 136
Telling Neighbors or Members of Your Faith Community 137
Sex Offender Registry 138

Chapter Nine: After Disclosure – What Now? 141
Boundaries and Agreements 143
Personal Healing: Self-Repair Through Internal Grounding 144
Managing Emotional States 147
Learn from the Past, Stay in the Present 150
How to Hold Someone Else Accountable 151
Holding Myself Accountable 152
Behavior Change Request 152
Rebuilding Trust 153
Ending the Relationship 156

Recommitment 156
Stay Positive 157
References 158

Chapter Ten: For Helping Professionals 159
Differences Between Addicted and Non-addicted Couples 159
The Role of the Therapist 162
How Long In Therapy 163
Crisis Intervention and Early Therapy 163
Beginning Repair Work 170
Special Areas of Concern for Therapists 171
  *Therapists Who Have Little or No Experience in
  Dealing with Sex Addiction 171*
  High-Risk Acting Out 171
  Other Areas of Safety 172
  Mismanaged Anger 174
  Premature Diagnosis 174
  Timing of Disclosure 175
  Use of Outside Monitoring and Polygraph 176
  Saving Face 177
  Countertransference 177
  Personal Sharing 177
  Don't Give Up Too Soon 178
Conclusions 178
References 179
Appendix 1: Frequently Asked Questions 181
Appendix 2: Recovery Resources 193
Index 197

Preface

It is our honor to write a preface to *Disclosing Secrets: An Addict's Guide for When, To Whom, and How Much to Reveal* and *Surviving Disclosure: A Partner's Guide for Healing the Betrayal of Intimate Trust*. No two people are better suited to write these tandem books than Dr. M. Deborah Corley and Dr. Jennifer Schneider. In 2002 they wrote *Disclosing Secrets*, a book which is still actively used by professionals working with those who have crossed inappropriate sexual boundaries.

In the book focused on disclosing, Drs. Corley and Schneider provide very specific and helpful step-by-step suggestions about if, when, and how to disclose. The book entitled, *Surviving Disclosure: A Partner's Guide for Healing the Betrayal of Intimate Trust* is a groundbreaking tool. It provides comprehensive and yet detailed information for partners facing the very difficult process of receiving a disclosure. Each book does a wonderful job of identifying the challenges facing each individual as well as the process of healing.

Those needing to disclose and their partners will appreciate Dr. Schneider and Dr. Corley creating two books with similar information. In a typically emotional process, knowing your partner is receiving similar information that is catered to their specific needs can be comforting and avert adding to the difficulty of the process. Readers will find the authors do not simply provide answers. Instead, those considering disclosing and whether to receive a disclosure are given multiple perspectives and case examples to aid them in deciding whether to proceed with the process of disclosure. Particularly helpful is the special emphasis throughout the books placed upon spouses or significant others, and children. The chapter entitled, "Reveal Now or Save the Worst for Later: The Pain of Staggered Disclosure" hits the nail on the head regarding very important information for the addict to address. They have done a wonderful job of integrating relevant research, clinical knowledge and case studies throughout these two books.

The authors go beyond simply addressing disclosure between two individuals and review other types of disclosures (e.g., a friend's spouse is having an affair) and special issues (e.g., sex offender registry) as well.

The books culminate with a chapter offering practical and direct information on what to do following disclosure, a piece often overlooked by those facing this process. The final chapter is for helping professionals. In addition to being a helpful tool for professionals, this particular chapter can be useful for those entering the process in finding a professional knowledgeable about disclosure or increasing the awareness of a trusted therapist. Each book has an appendix addressing frequently asked questions, providing a tremendous resource for both therapists and clients. Dr. Corley and Dr. Schneider have left no stone unturned in their effort to create a safe and humane process for disclosing very difficult and painful information.

At Psychological Counseling Services, we shall provide these books as a tool for clients. One provides a road map for those needing to disclose and supports them in having the courage to do so through a detailed and caring process. The other provides partners who are understandably hurt, angry, and confused, the information and support they desperately need to negotiate the process of disclosure. Dr. Schneider and Dr. Corley provide much needed information to limit the trauma associated with the disclosure process. We want to thank Deborah Corley and Jennifer Schneider for providing a carefully thought through and sensitive resource for the general public as well as professionals.

Marcus R. Earle, Ph.D., LMFT, CSAT
Ralph H. Earle, M.Div., Ph.D., LMFT, A.B.P.P., CSAT

Introduction

Over a decade ago, we wrote a workbook on disclosure for addicts and their partners. After feedback from therapists, addicted persons, and partners, we decided that we wanted to have a book for addicts and a separate one for partners because the experience of disclosure is so different for each.

This book is written for people whose mates (the addicts) have been keeping secrets that they are now ready or are being encouraged to reveal. It is also a guidebook for healing from the trauma of disclosure and the addiction. It also contains information for the partner about how to decide whether to stay or leave a relationship. For those who decide to stay, it talks about how to repair and grow a relationship after disclosure. The companion book for addicts – *Disclosing Secrets: An Addict's Guide to When, To Whom & How Much to Disclose* is available at amazon.com

Revealing his or her behavior is often very difficult for the addict, but it can be devastating for the partner who is on the receiving end. Much thought, care, and planning should go into any disclosure, although in reality the initial disclosure is often unplanned. The meaning of disclosure is different for the partner or other recipients of such information than it is for the addict. It can be very traumatic for the partner and recovery can take a long time. Behaviors that are illegal or put at risk the health or the finances of a household or company make the timeliness of telling even more important. Matters are complicated further by the number and ages of children, the state of finances and health, years invested in a marriage, if someone's sexual orientation is suddenly revealed and especially if other children are the result of sexual behavior outside the marriage. However, a disclosure indefinitely postponed or thoughtlessly carried out can be as destructive as the addictive behavior itself. Admission of relapse has its own set of problems for the partner, reopening old wounds and further damaging trust, yet not disclosing the relapse can prove fatal to the relationship once the behavior is discovered. We hope that this book will help you navigate these difficult waters.

Of the many people who donated their time and energy to complete surveys and interviews in our earlier research and to those in our most recent study, we are grateful. The participants were partners of those recovering from substance use disorders, food addiction, out-of-control spending, old-fashioned sex addiction as well as Internet and cybersex addiction, and other psychiatric disorders. Unfortunately, when sexual behaviors outside the relationship are involved, it is especially difficult for the partner not to take it personally; emotional and psychological trauma to the partner and loss of self-esteem are likely consequences. This is why this book includes the impact of disclosure about all addictions including sexual addiction. Nonetheless, we believe that you, our readers, will find the book useful no matter what your partner's addiction history. In fact, people who are not partners of addicts but would benefit from receiving healthy disclosure of a secret such as a child out of wedlock or childhood abuse will also find this book helpful.

Both men and women can become addicted. Most of the time, we use the words addict and partner to denote two people in a coupled relationship. If a pronoun is used to identify the addict, we may use either he or she, but most often we use he. If we refer to the partner, we often use she or he, but most often we use she. We mean for this book to help people in all types of relationships, not just those in a heterosexual marriage. We use the term relationship, coupleship, and marital relationship to reflect a committed relationship that exists or is being formulated between two people. We try to make a distinction if we are talking about a parent-child relationship, patient-physician, supervisor-employee, or some other type of specific relationship.

If you and your mate have been in recovery for a while, you have undoubtedly already experienced revelation of secrets. As a result of your reaction, your mate (the addict) may have many fears and may be ambivalent about again disclosing. This book will provide you with a blueprint for receiving further admissions. You will have a better awareness of the support you and your mate (the addict) need during what feels like the worst days of your life. Things will get better but it takes a while.

The book is organized into three sections. The first section, Chapters One through Four, looks at the power of disclosure – the uncertainty, anxiety and suspicions you may have lived with, the horror, pain, anger, and self-doubt the revelations call forth in the recipient, along with the validation of your concerns the information brings, and the healing power of the truth – examining a variety of situations where people have been lied to and were not told secrets, but are now facing receiving painful information. This section discusses why people choose to come clean, the wide range of reactions and consequences, and how to determine what type of disclosure is right for you.

The middle section, Chapters Five through Eight, tell you how to go about participating in a variety of types of disclosures. Chapter Five outlines a step-by-step approach to doing a formal disclosure including what, if anything, is best kept private. Most people have questions about what to tell the children – even adult children – and that information is in Chapter Six. It is common for addicted people to relapse, and acknowledgment of a slip or relapse is a serious issue. Chapter Seven provides tips for what to do when there is a relapse, how to handle other admissions when the addict remembers something else, setting and maintaining boundaries, testing for sexually transmitted diseases, atonement, and coping. Finally, Chapter Eight speaks to special issues that sometimes exist and decisions that need to be made about what to say at work, what to do if the media gets involved, or what to tell people in your faith community or others outside your immediate family.

In the final section, Chapters Nine and Ten tell you how to proceed after receiving a disclosure as well as how a therapist can best help you with the process. You will also learn what do to if you or your mate (the addict) wants a period of separation, and how to deal with your anger, despair, and other strong emotions. This chapter also provides suggestions for healing and forgiveness. Every situation provides an opportunity to be one's best self and learn from the experience. Ways to learn the lessons are located in this chapter.

The final chapter, Chapter Ten, is really for professionals who are helping addicted persons and their partners work through the process of disclosure. Although we believe this book will help any partner with this process, disclosure often generates strong emotions that not everyone is able to manage. We strongly encourage you to seek the help of a trained professional to help you. If you are already working with someone, this chapter may be of help to them.

Although this book is for all people in recovery, we offer material specific to sexual addiction in the two appendices in the back. Appendix A contains Frequently Asked Questions about Disclosing Sexual Secrets while Appendix B lists Recovery Resources. Excruciating as disclosure is, it's a process that can strengthen and even improve a relationship. Disclosing secrets is always difficult. With this book, the process can become an opportunity for healing. We hope you will take that opportunity now.

JPS and MDC

Chapter One

The Power of Disclosure: Why Addicts Disclose and Why Partners Need Disclosure

Jay, a previously married 40-year-old salesman had had a string of affairs along with cocaine use; his first wife eventually left him. He hoped to do better by Monica, but within a year of their wedding he had already racked up two brief affairs. He rationalized that his problem "wasn't all that bad, he could control things" because he used only alcohol, not cocaine, during the short-term affairs. The crisis came after three years of marriage, when Sue, his latest affair partner, threatened to tell Monica about the relationship. Jay decided to tell Monica before she would hear the bad news from Sue. Monica was devastated. Knowing about Jay's history of cheating in his first marriage, she asked him about any other affairs during their three years together, and was distraught to learn that there had been two others.

Monica and Jay's marriage survived his affairs and excessive drinking with the help of addiction counseling, couples' therapy, and Twelve-Step mutual-help meetings for sex addicts and for partners. Years later, remembering the anger and pain she'd felt at learning of Jay's affairs, Monica recalled that the *single most important factor that made her willing to stay* in the marriage was Jay's decision to disclose his secret to her before she heard it from Sue. What this decision meant to Monica was that she and their marriage were important enough to Jay that he would tell her his secret. He was willing to risk losing her in order to save the marriage, and this was very powerful to Monica.

This book is about secrets kept by addicts and about the effects of these secrets on the partners. It is also about the secrets parents, children, friends, and others keep in hopes that if no one talks about the secret, it doesn't exist. This book is also about *lies*, which protect secrets; about *disclosure*, which is how people reveal secrets; and about *forgiveness*, which is how painful secrets, once revealed, get processed and ultimately lose their ability to wound.

Not all secrets are bad. Secrets can sometimes enhance intimacy and protect life. A mate who chooses to share something special and private about himself that no one else knows makes you feel special and can strengthen the bond between you. Intimacy is the willingness to be vulnerable to another person, to open up to him or her knowing that your partner has your best interest at heart. Transparency is the basis of connections. Sometimes, however, not telling a secret is the kindest and most appropriate thing to do when someone's physical or emotional health is fragile or if the person lacks the intellectual capacity or maturity to understand the information. It is also wise to keep a secret when revealing it risks violence. But most people keep secrets because they are afraid. They fear that if the truth is known, something bad will happen, such as that the partner will leave them or shame them.

Yet people do decide to disclose.

Why Addicts Disclose

Sometimes addicts disclose because they feel so ashamed and guilty that the guilt overwhelms them, so they tell. Others are forced to tell because some authority (such as the law, a boss, a friend, or a therapist) insists on it, and they figure it is better to do damage control than have the partner hear about their addiction from someone else. Sometimes people tell because they think it is the right thing to do—they are trying to be congruent with their values, and deep down, they value honesty over lying even if they haven't always told the truth. This is especially true for people who are in addiction recovery and are trying to rebuild the relationship on a foundation of honesty or when starting new relationships. By opening up in a heartfelt way, the addict honors the partner and knows that the partner can now make a choice based on truth and honesty. The partner in turn is likely to feel relieved and more hopeful.

Other addicts break under the intense scrutiny of a partner, therapist, employer, or police and tell because they are tired of keeping the lie or don't see any other way out.

In cases in which a partner's health could be harmed with a sexually transmitted disease, if financial consequences are imminent, or if a pregnancy from another relationship outside the marriage is a possibility, then disclosure is a must. Addicts tell because they feel they owe it to their partners. Protecting their partner from a health risk is more important than are other consequences for telling.

Like Jay in the example above, some people tell because they got caught or someone else threatened to tell. Sometimes they feel they have no choice, or they tell out of obedience or because they hope this will be the end of the pain they are experiencing as a result of carrying the burden of the secret.

Others tell because they are members of a Twelve-Step program of recovery, a program that recommends rigorous honesty as a cornerstone of sobriety. Yet sometimes the advice from the Twelve- Step program is a bit confusing, leaving the addict wondering whether to acknowledge his compulsive behavior. In our companion book, *Disclosing Secrets: An Addict's Guide for When, To Whom, and How Much to Reveal* you can read at length about what Twelve-Step books advise the addict about disclosure and how this is best played out in the couple relationship.

Some addicts reveal only the minimum or only what they believe their partner already knows or is very likely to find out. Others tell everything, or all the information that their partner asks for. Still others divulge the basic behaviors but not the details. Each of these choices has different consequences for the addict and the partner. (In Chapter 5, we will provide specific information on how to disclose as well as samples of disclosures.)

Why Partners Need Disclosure

The American public has been taught over and over again that although misconduct is bad, the deception that it often engenders in an attempt to avoid discovery is worse. In 1974 President Nixon was forced out of office following the Watergate episode not because of what his aides did, but rather because of his complicity in the cover up. In 1998 President Clinton was impeached by the U. S. House of Representatives on charges of perjury and obstruction of justice after lying to members of Congress and a grand jury about having an inappropriate sexual relationship. In 2011 Congressman Anthony Weiner was forced to resign from Congress not because he emailed sexual letters and photos of himself to young women, but because he repeatedly lied to his friends, Congressional associates, and his constituency.

The same is true in personal relationships. If your mate has had an affair (or several) or has been involved in other extramarital sexual activities you will likely find it harder to recover from the secrets and the repeated deception than from the behavior itself. Repeated dishonesty is traumatizing. Partners *want* to believe what their mate tells them, often ignoring their instincts which tell them that something is wrong. Faced again and again with a discrepancy between what your gut says and what the addict says, you may come to feel as if you are crazy. You may find it difficult to trust your own judgment and conclusions. Moreover, you cannot make informed decisions about your life because you are not in possession of all the facts. By the time the truth is out, you may have become a trauma victim. If so, you are a victim at least as much of the emotional abuse of deception as of the addict's behaviors.

Survival of the relationship in the aftermath of secrets and lies depends more than anything else on the addict's ongoing honesty. And the first step to this new behavior is the disclosure, painful though it might be. As described in the vignette at the beginning of this chapter, it was Jay's willingness to be honest despite the risk of losing Monica that made Monica willing to give the relationship a chance and to stick around to see if real changes would happen. Disclosure and honesty are the keystones for the partner to recover from the trauma of having lived in a web of lies practiced by the person she had loved and trusted. Without honesty, the partner can experience individual recovery with the help of therapy and a support group, but the relationship will not survive.

When Laurie, 34, a nurse and mother of two young children, discovered her husband Todd's secret sexual life on the computer, she related,

> *I felt total distrust in myself, my spouse, and the relationship. I felt betrayed, confused, afraid, and stunned. The person I loved and trusted most in the world had lied about who he was. I felt I had lived through a vast and sinister cover-up.*

THE POWER OF DISCLOSURE

As we said before, learning in one way or another about the addict's behaviors and cover-up is very stressful, often traumatic for the partner. Partners typically begin obsessively reviewing the history of the relationship. Endless questions are likely to pop into your head: *How could he do this to me? How could I have not known this? What else did he do? Did he expose me to an STD? Was it my fault? Are my children at risk? How can I prevent this from happening again? How will I ever trust him again?* Anger, fear, self-doubt, pain over the loss of the "relationship-I-thought-I-had", distrust, shame, self-blame, depression – can overwhelm you. Intrusive thoughts may race through your head. You may become so preoccupied with them that it is difficult to focus on what you are supposed to be doing. You may feel that you need to know more and more in order to understand the past and avoid future pain. To this end, you may repeatedly search through his computer files, portable electronic devices, and belongings, attempt to keep careful track of his whereabouts, and engage in other "detective" activities. These are all normal, a natural consequences of the trauma you have experienced.

All too often, though, these expected reactions are intensified by the partner's own prior experiences. An example from another slice of life relates to soldiers who develop post-traumatic stress disorder (PTSD) as a result of what they went through in wartime. Among a group of soldiers who had similar experiences in Viet Nam or Iran or Afghanistan, why did some develop PTSD while others didn't? There are surely many reasons related to each soldier's individual experience in battle, but research has shown that people most vulnerable to PTSD are those who earlier in their lives, often in childhood, went through other traumatic events. Similarly, partners who grew up in dysfunctional families where they may have received inadequate nurturing, were not allowed to express their feelings, had parents who had one addiction or another, may have been physically or sexually or emotionally abused, were physically or emotionally abandoned by one parent or another, or were basically left to their own devices, developed coping strategies that increased their subsequent vulnerability to PTSD.

Children are normally egocentric, and thus tend to blame themselves for bad things that happen around them. A young child who is not treated with love comes to believe that the reason is that she is not lovable. If so, it must be because she is not a worthwhile person.

A child is likely to feel responsible for a worsening situation at home, and feels guilty over her inability to make things better. She may worry constantly about what others will think, try to figure out what they want and go to extraordinary lengths to give it them. Her self-esteem may come from being a people-pleaser. She becomes very sensitive to the mood of important adults. These characteristics, when carried into adulthood, have been called *codependency*. They include:

- feeling you are not a worthwhile person
- neglecting your own needs and desires while focusing on others'
- denying the seriousness of problems in your life
- feeling responsible for someone else's behavior
- setting boundaries or agreements but not following through with consequences
- accepting sexual attention when you want love
- substituting intensity in the relationship for intimacy
- making excuses for his behavior and covering up for him
- rescuing him
- believing you can control another person and make him change
- avoiding confronting him on his behaviors for fear he will reject or leave you
- remaining in harmful situations too long

For the partner who has grown up with codependent beliefs and behaviors – and many people in relationship with addicts have done so – the trauma of learning about the behavior is exacerbated and can actually result in development of a post-traumatic stress disorder (PTSD). This is why seeing a knowledgeable counselor and getting help for yourself is so important. We will discuss this in greater detail in Chapter Nine

Honesty—Not Just for Addicts

There is no doubt that both unplanned and planned disclosures can be very painful for the partner and initially can have multiple negative consequences. Yet our research has shown that looking back, both addicts and partners overwhelmingly believe that disclosure was the right thing to do, that it benefited them and their relationship.

The Bible says that the truth will set you free (John 8:32). All religions value honesty as a character trait and expect honesty as a sign of a covenant (a binding or solemn agreement). Honesty is part of being trustworthy and trustworthiness is one of the most widely desired characteristics of a potential partner in a relationship (Gottman, 2011). In most marriages the covenant of honesty is usually an expectation, even if not voiced.

For many addicts, admitting the whole truth for the first time, although extremely difficult, feels like a kind of freedom. For the first time, they no longer have to hide, hold their breath, or wait for the next shoe to drop. They no longer have to live a double life. They can begin to breathe again. They no longer have to feel guilty. This freedom is the power of disclosure. Of course, how they feel depends also on the consequences of telling, but over time most addicts report that, despite the consequences, they are glad they told. Even a larger percentage of partners report they are glad the addict told.

All addicts who are holding onto a major face a dilemma of when and how much to tell. When the secret is sexual, keeping it secret can be very destructive. Frank Pittman, in *Private Lies* (1989), defines *infidelity* as "a breach of the trust, a betrayal of a relationship, a breaking of an agreement." However, infidelity isn't only about the sexual behavior itself: The dishonesty about the infidelity involves loss of self-esteem, breaking an important commitment to you and to your relationship, and the energy of keeping the secret that the addict takes away from the relationship. Pittman states that dishonesty may be a greater violation of the rules than the affair or misconduct, and acknowledges that more marriages end as a result of maintaining the secret than do in the wake of telling. He speculates that the partner may be angry, but will be angrier if the affair continues and you find out later. Our research has supported this speculation. We found that the betrayal felt by partners is as much about the lying and secret keeping as about the actual behavior. We also learned that the best chance that a relationship will survive compulsive sexual behavior is if the addict becomes honest and transparent. This is especially true when the behavior disclosed constitutes a relapse.

Although not all addicts are sex addicts or have been sexually unfaithful, they have been unfaithful in that the drug or gambling or other addictive behavior becomes the primary relationship in their lives. It is as if the person has an affair with the drug. It becomes the most important thing in his or her life and the addict will put the drug or behavior before marriage, family, job, community, and all other meaningful relationships.

Emily Brown (1991) concurs that, in most circumstances, the unfaithful person must tell the partner if healing is to occur. When an affair remains secret, all communication about other matters is gradually impaired. The same is true when the affair is with a drug. Ms. Brown advises that behaviors from previous relationships or from long ago do not always have to be revealed. She agrees with our assessment that before actual rebuilding of the relationship can occur, time and support for the partner are necessary and that therapy sessions often take longer or are more frequent to help the partner express her or his anger and sadness about the infidelity, no matter if it has been via a sexual encounter, drugs, or other addictive behavior.

An addict's important motivation for disclosing addictive behaviors to the partner is a desire to salvage the relationship. When the partner recognizes that this is addict's motivation, the disclosure can be the first step to rebuilding trust for the couple.

If you recall Jay and Monica, whose story began this chapter, Jay decided to come clean with Monica about his affair with Sue after Sue threatened to tell Monica herself. Jay weighed the risks and benefits of disclosure and decided he had a better chance to save the marriage if Monica heard the bad news directly from him rather than from his affair partner. Upon learning of the affair, Monica had a mixture of reactions, among them anger, hurt, and the painful realization that she would have to construct a new picture in her head of the reality of her recent relationship with Jay. A series of confusing events came to her mind, and she recognized that Jay's ongoing affair might have contributed to the confusion.

For example, Monica remembered a recent excursion with Jay to the Great Smoky Mountains, a vacation she'd really looked forward to but which turned into an emotional disaster. Monica loved hiking and camping, and Jay, who was a city guy at heart, had agreed to spend a long weekend with Monica in the mountains. She felt particularly warm and loving to him at the start of that weekend, and kept telling him how much she loved him—but every attempt to get close to him physically or emotionally was rebuffed by Jay. In fact, he seemed to be going out of his way to be particularly cruel and unpleasant to her. Monica kept wondering all weekend what she had done wrong.

Now, having learned about the affair, Monica asked Jay about what had been going on for him at the time of the camping trip. Reluctantly, he told her he'd been at the height of his affair with Sue, wishing every second that he was with his lover rather than her. Every loving word or gesture by Monica increased Jay's guilt. He kept thinking, "If she only knew what I'm thinking, she wouldn't think I'm such a caring wonderful husband, she'd realize I'm really worthless." By his uncaring behaviors all weekend, Jay was subconsciously trying to prove to Monica that he didn't deserve her love and positive regard.

Hearing the truth from Jay, painful though it was for her, helped Monica make sense of the recent events in their marriage and *validated for her that she wasn't crazy* and that her reactions to Jay had been normal. Jay was clearly unhappy to be grilled about these events, but his willingness to answer all her questions suggested to Monica, even in the midst of her anger and pain, that he was committed to their relationship and willing to experience great discomfort in order to try to save the marriage. The power of disclosure is that it gave Monica hope that they might somehow rebuild trust and restore their relationship.

References

Alcoholics Anonymous. New York: Alcoholics Anonymous World Services, Inc., 1953.
Anonymous. *Hope and Recovery: A Twelve Step Guide for Healing from Compulsive Sexual Behavior.* Cnter City, Minn., 1987.
Brown, Emily. *Patterns of Infidelity.* New York: Brunner Mazel, 1991

Carnes, Stephanie (Ed). *Mending a Shattered Heart: A Guide for Partners of Sex Addicts.* Carefree, AZ: Gentle Path Press, Second Edition, 2011.

Gottman, John. *The Science of Trust: Emotional Attunement for Couples.* New York: W.W.Norton, 2011.

Pittman, Frank. *Private Lies. New York: WW Norton Co., 1989.*

Schneider, Jennifer, Corley, Deborah M., and Irons, Richard. Surviving disclosure of infidelity: Result of an international survey of 164 recovering sex addicts and partners. *Sexual Addiction & Compulsivity* 5:189-218, 1998.

Schneider, Jennifer and Schneider, Burt. *Sex, Lies, and Forgiveness: Couples. Speak on Healing from Sex Addiction.* 3rd ed. Tucson, Ariz.: Recovery

Resources Press, Third Edition, 2004.

Chapter Two

Secrets and Lies: Lies Influence Relationships, and Relationships Influence Lies

Why do people lie—that seems pretty obvious doesn't it? They don't want to get in trouble. But it is not that simple for most. Some people speculate that addicts are born liars, but that is not true. We all learn to lie through an important developmental process in which lying serves a specific purpose.

In his book *Lies, Lies, Lies: The Psychology of Deceit* (1996), Charles Ford, MD cites several studies that demonstrate how children use lying. He summarizes:

> *Lying is . . . an essential component in the process of developing autonomy and differentiating oneself from one's parents. The capacity to fool parents demonstrates to children that parents are not omnipotent . . . lying is reinforced (positively or negatively) by the degree to which the child is rewarded or punished for deceitful behavior. (p. 86)*

As children become older, lying provides a way for them to learn that their parents can't totally control them. In this way, the child gains a sense of autonomy. In another example, Ford explains that children use lying to help them in other ways beyond the developmental task of separating self from parents/others. This important distinction relates to an addict's and partner's experiences:

> *If the child experiences repeated trauma (such as sexual abuse, physical abuse, or being raised in a family with an alcoholic parent), lying may become one way to cope with stress. Certainly, putting*

on a false face appears to be one coping mechanism learned when growing up in a family with alcoholism. (p 86)

Clearly, lying serves an important developmental function as well as a means for coping. Unfortunately, without help most addicts and partners fail to learn other ways to gain autonomy and independence in relationships or cope well with adversity or trauma.

Of course, there are other reasons people lie. As we mentioned in Chapter 1, a major reason is to avoid punishment or to punish someone when you are angry. Fooling someone else makes you feel powerful or that you are a part of something. When someone doesn't feel they can ever live up to the expectations of others, that person might lie as a form of self-deception, to maintain their self-esteem, or to accommodate the other person's self-deception. A lie can resolve role conflict or help create a sense of identity. Many times people lie about how they feel to avoid acknowledging the pain they are in.

To keep a secret, you must tell a lie. A lie is a deliberate act in which you either misrepresent or conceal information. There are lies of omission and commission (deliberate lies). There are lies you tell yourself and lies that you tell others. There are lies that are justifiable—for example, to avoid offending someone or to prepare a surprise party for a friend—and there are lies that are toxic. Toxic lies are those addicts and partners use to keep others from learning about their dark side. Toxic lies also violate one's values, ethics, morals, and spiritual beliefs.

As the partner, you can sense or feel the anxiety created by the addict's need to keep you from finding out the secret. Although you may not be sure about what is going on, your gut reaction tells you there is something wrong. However, the more you ask, beg, nag, threaten, snoop, or doubt, the more the addict denies and the more you obsess about finding out what is wrong. You sometimes catch part of the lie, but the addict is so clever about covering one lie with another, you are never totally sure what the truth is. In an attempt to figure this out, you obsess about it for hours on end. The obsessing crowds your head, taking up valuable hours each day and night, causing loss of productivity by day, insomnia by night. Gradually it builds a wall between you and your mate as it erodes your self-confidence and faith in yourself.

This chapter illustrates several types of secrets guarded by various types of lies and how partners use and fear the secrets and lies that influence their relationships.

Several Types of Secrets

Secrets that hurt relationships are as common and numerous as are people. Here are a few types of commonly kept secrets that are often triggers for partners and addicts.

The Emotional Secret

Most addicts and many partners of addicts were raised in families with emotionally dismissing or disapproving parents. Disapproving parents disregard, ignore, or trivialize a child's negative emotions. Disapproving parents say, "Don't feel—all feelings require something of me that I don't have to give or don't know how to give, so don't feel. If you have a feeling, I will ignore it or tell you it isn't that important." Consequently these children grow up unable to identify the feelings they or others have, or discount their own feeling states.

Dismissing parents reprimand or punish children for emotional expressions. Similar to the disapproving parent, these parents also cannot tolerate the child having an emotional state that they can't control, so the child's response to emotional situations is shut down by threats or punishment. A common response would be, "You better stop that crying before I give you something to cry about!" or "Stop that crying – that cut doesn't hurt!"

Research shows that children raised with these types of parents grow up having a hard time trusting their own judgment. This makes sense. If children are told that their feelings are wrong—that they really don't feel the way they say they feel, —then they are likely to grow up believing there is something inherently wrong with them. Unfortunately, the result is someone who can't tolerate emotional distress in himself, herself, or others.

Take Martha who is married to Michael. Martha was raised in an alcoholic family and suffered from low self-esteem. Her father's rages during drinking left her and her siblings afraid to show any emotions.

If he was raging, she did everything possible to disappear. She remembered once when her sister started to cry while her father was raging. Her father picked up her sister, slapped her hard across the face, and then shook her for what seemed like forever while yelling for her sister to stop crying. Martha quickly learned it wasn't safe to show any emotions around her father.

When her father wasn't drinking, Martha tried to be the best she could in hopes that she could prevent him from drinking and her mother from getting depressed. Hoping to somehow get her parents to stop their crazy behaviors, she did everything she could to be the "perfect" child. She tried out for school plays and was always given a part, but both parents were too busy to attend. She studied hard in school and was at the top of her class, yet neither of her parents attended her college graduation where she was valedictorian.

Martha felt that no matter what she did, it was not good enough to deserve their love. Working constantly to keep her feelings in check, she behaved kindly to everyone, no matter what they did to her. But before long, she noticed that the people she seemed to attract took advantage of her, asking her to do things that were beyond her capability or her wishes. She continually struggled with her feelings of resentment and frustration that others were taking advantage of her, but feared that if she said anything, they would abandon her. Sometimes, though, when the stress overwhelmed her, she would eat with a vengeance: ice cream, donuts, potato chips—whatever she could get her hands on, bingeing until she thought she'd burst. Then she'd feel so guilty for the feelings and for eating so much that she'd make herself throw up and then run several miles in a day or take laxatives to make sure she did not gain weight. She remembered how when she was a child, her mother complained that she was too fat. Her response was to try even harder to please everyone.

Martha was very surprised when Michael, a medical resident from the hospital where she worked part time, asked her out. She couldn't believe that this good-looking intelligent man from a prominent Jewish family would be interested in her.

Martha saw Michael as a sensitive doctor, caring for others, kind and gentle. He did not drink much and was a hard worker—he would be able to provide for her and their children. He was committed to his faith and felt strongly that their children be raised the same way. Although her family was not very religious, she longed to belong to a religion and hoped that Michael's faith could be her own. As the wife of a doctor, perhaps her parents would finally think she had done well.

Michael had been raised by emotionally dismissing parents. As a child he was thin and shy. Often last to be chosen on the team, he was frequently taunted and sometimes picked on by the bullies at school. When he would come home crying, he was told to stop acting like a sissy, to stop crying and "be a man." His father was famous for telling him that there was something wrong with him because Michael cried when his dog was hit by a car—that it was just a dog. Michael was then told the story of his father's family's experience during the Holocaust and that Michael was just a spoiled baby trying to use tears to get his way instead of minding his father. Early in his life, Michael vowed never to cry or let himself feel anything again.

Michael was drawn to Martha like a moth to a flame. People are commonly drawn to mates who they think will provide for them what they missed in childhood. Here was Martha, kind to all the patients, attentive to his stories—laughing and enthusiastic about everything. This clearly was a woman he wanted to marry. She was interested in his work and understanding of his work schedule. She seemed to have no problem rearranging her schedule to fit his so they could be together. She was pretty, smart, and a hard worker herself. She even agreed to raise their children in the Jewish faith. Surely this would please his father.

So Michael and Martha got married. But Michael soon found that his work schedule did not leave much time to be with Martha. After the children were born, she began to focus increasingly on them and complain more and more about why he wasn't home more. He didn't know why she could not see the stress he was under or hear the demands the hospital was making of him. In the meantime, Martha grew increasingly resentful that she had given up everything of importance to her for him. She saw him working more and more, while being less and less available to her and the children. In the past he at least complained about the demands of work, but he no longer even shared that with her. All he did was demand that the family appear perfect in the community. Unable to talk about her fear that she was no longer important to him, she put all her energy into the children and her volunteer activities. She wanted to punish Michael for his rigidity and isolating behavior, but he would never listen to her unless she was raging. Eventually she would just blow up and shut herself off from him. He would walk out of the house and she would eat to make herself feel better. Then she would put her fingers down her throat, vomiting to keep herself below the petite 95 pounds Michael said he liked.

What a painful existence for both Martha and Michael! Martha's eating disorder was out of control; Michael's work addiction had not been the solution and an affair with an intern was about to make things even worse. As you see, they both feared the same thing—that they were not important to the other person. If each had been able to talk about the pain they were in or hear the other, perhaps they would have been able to create solutions.

Keeping secrets about how they really feel emotionally is a component of all secret-keeping for both addicts and partners. This type of secret is usually the one that people are least concerned about, but for most is a catalyst to engage in some behavior that is not good for them or the relationship. Stopping this type of secret keeping is the key to obtaining emotional competence.

The Secret That Isn't a Secret—the Elephant in the Living Room

Sometimes secrets are known, but the unspoken (or sometimes even spoken) rule is to pretend they don't exist. KEEP QUIET, don't rock the boat, don't bring attention to the elephant in the living room. Then you don't have to face the situation. An example is what happens to children in families in which there is ongoing addiction or domestic violence. The children see Mom drunk or simply "not there," perhaps because she is using prescription drugs. Or they see Dad hit the older brother so hard that his nose and mouth bleed and then hear Dad tell him "this is for your own good." These children often pretend that nothing out of the ordinary is happening; they make it their job to do whatever it takes to keep the secret hidden for fear matters will get worse if they tell. They don't invite friends over, fearing that the friends will discover the truth about their family. They learn to discount their feelings, and to carry on conversations in which nothing important is ever discussed. They find ways to hide evidence, and frequently take on adult responsibilities far beyond their years. This type of secret-keeping influences both the day-to-day relationships within the family and external relationships.

The normal, healthy development of a child includes opportunities for the child to experience painful and confusing situations. What makes the difference is when a caring adult helps the child identify the feelings he or she is having, validates the feelings, and then helps the child figure out what to do and how to take steps to feel better. But in families where secrets are kept at all costs, children grow up unable to tolerate emotional discomfort. Boundaries are often overly controlling or extremely chaotic, and children have little emotional competence. Later on, such people usually attract someone with a complementary style of relating, so it is no surprise that many addicts choose a partner who is an adult child of an addict or victim of some type of abuse or neglect. Such relationships are very likely to quickly include secrets: Each member of the couple lacks the skills to cope with addiction and codependent traits, and keeping secrets is already a part of how the couple relates.

Most people think addicts lie more than partners or that addicts lie to everybody and partners only lie to themselves. Examine below the reasons why partners lie and see what you think. Can you think of other reasons why you have lied?

Partners' Lies

Partners tell lies to others to cover up their shame about the addict's behavior. Yet, the partner lies to herself first to be able to lie to others. In her book *When Your Lover Is a Liar*, Susan Forward identifies six common lies women tell themselves. Codependent partners use all of them—see which ones you have used.

He Would Never Lie to Me.

This is used by partners who are basically honest and believe that everyone else is too. This lie is particularly true of the naïve partner who is new to a relationship or marriage. They have little experience with betrayal, so often are not as aware that something is not right in the relationship as partners who grew up in families in which betrayal was a norm.

The partner new to recovery may hear the addict profess at self-help meetings that he shares the value of honesty, but notices that at home, her mate is very different. The discrepancy between the public and the private is the "red flag" that all is not right in the relationship. Yet believing he would never lie to her, this partner may stay stuck in denial until very serious consequences happen.

Maybe He Lied to Other [Women] People, but He Wouldn't Lie to Me.

This lie is common in situations in which the addict has been open about his previous addictive behavior or acting out. During the courtship stage, with the best of intentions, the addict kept a lid on his old addictive behaviors, but over time, they re-emerged. Despite seeing and hearing evidence that her mate has slipped or relapsed, the partner tells herself that he is different now. Because he trusted her enough to tell about the past, she tells herself that he won't lie now.

Yes, He Lies, but He Loves Me and That's All That Matters.

Some people are so desperate for love that they will submit to various forms of abuse in an effort to win or keep a relationship. When someone says "I love you" to a desperate person, the person interprets that to mean there is a relationship—a future—someone cares. We see this lie in partners of all types of addicts, who settle for less because they believe the relationship they have is better than none at all. More times than not, the partner using this type of lie doesn't have a clue what love or friendship really is.

This lie is also the favorite lie of partners who begin an affair with a married man and believe that somehow their relationship is special and that someday he will leave his wife for her. She believes his explanation that his wife doesn't want to have sex anymore, that he doesn't love his wife, and that she (the affair partner) is the most important person in his life. She lies to herself and says it must be true. She waits for his call on weekends and holidays in case he can "get away" for a secret phone call or a few moments for quick sex or sexual talk. Her efforts to be always available to him result in her shutting herself off from her friends. She becomes progressively more isolated and dependent on the lover.

Yes, He Lies, but He's a Victim of Circumstances.

Even if the addict was a victim, his victimizing you is not justified. Having empathy is important in any relationship, but no one has the right to hurt another to try to make themselves feel better. There are better ways to cope.

Yes, He Lies, but I Can Fix Him.

Many addicts and partners come from homes in which one or both parents were also addicted, forcing the child to take on adult or care-taking roles too early in life. It is no surprise that this lie is used often. Of course the partner has a secondary gain for being in the "fixing" mode—you have the illusion of control and the crisis keeps the relationship in enough chaos that you don't have to face the reality that there are real problems with the way both of you behave.

In a common scenario the wife covers for the husband who is out drinking while she waits for him in her party dress. She tells the friend or family member on the phone that he isn't feeling well, so they won't be there at the party.

Sometimes partners feel they have to cover for the addict at his job. They justify this lie by saying, "His boss won't understand that he just had a slip. It is okay that I lie to the boss for him—otherwise he will lose his job and then what will happen to me and the kids?" Ultimately the partner thinks, "If I pretend all is well, then I don't have to face the fact that this marriage is a mess and I am stuck."

Yes, He Lies, but It's My Fault.

For those who care-take too much, the other side is taking on the blame for the addict's behavior. A favorite method addicts have for manipulating the situation is to try to convince you that their out-of-control behavior is your fault. Partners get caught up in the cycle of trying to fix things, feeling that they did something wrong. Wake up! You can't *make* anyone lie. You can't force words to come out of his mouth. You can't fix him no matter how hard you try to remedy the situation.

Partners also tell lies of omission. For example, you may feel angry and scared. When your mate asks what is wrong, you say "nothing," not wanting to rock the boat for fear that he will act out again. Or when others see that you are not doing well, you falsely reassure them that everything is fine. Maybe you go to the doctor for help because you haven't been sleeping. She asks you if you are having problems with your marriage and you report "not really," rather than telling her the evidence you have found about your mate.

Partners also minimize the seriousness of the problem when shame is attached to the addictive behavior. This is common when an addict goes to treatment for cocaine and sex addiction. The partner often tells others only about the cocaine addiction.

Disclosing a secret sometimes leads to favorable results, but sometimes results in devastating consequences. Finding out someone is keeping secrets throws the relationship into turmoil. Either way, the process of creating, keeping, telling, and hearing the secret alters the relationship in very important ways.

Many addicts say they lie and resist disclosure because they don't want to hurt their partner. That stance shows little respect for you. Our research shows that over 90% of partners wanted to be told the truth because they were made to feel crazy—as if the reality they were seeing did not exist. Despite the pain, they felt better about being told. The next chapter discusses the consequences of telling, the good, bad and ugly.

References

Ford, Charles. *Lies, Lies, Lies: The Psychology of Deceit*. Arlington, VA: American Psychiatric Publishing, Inc.1999

Forward, Susan. *When Your Lover is a Liar*. New York: HarperCollins, 1999.

Chapter Three

Is Disclosure Right for You? If, When, and How Much to Ask the Addict

Disclosures come in all forms; some are done with integrity and some are done in the worst way possible. Obviously, if you are reading this book your mate has said something about a formal disclosure, is considering disclosure, has disclosed to someone, or has disclosed to you and you and are looking for ways to make things easier and better.

It is safe to say that all revelations are painful and difficult for everyone, but probably hardest on you. You will receive information that may reinforce your suspicions, be a total shock, be more than you even wanted to know, or will leave you wanting to know more. It may be the straw that breaks your relationship's back. Yet, most partners and addicts (over 90% in our study) report they are glad the disclosure happened. This high approval and the fact that most couples did not split up after disclosure (see Chapter 4) led us to think that the couples who had acknowledged the secrets had a better chance of saving the relationship than those who had not.

When the disclosure is done with integrity, both the addict and partner may experience a kind of relief. The addicted person feels a sense of freedom from the secret life and relief from the shame. The partner may experience a wide variety of other feelings, but also often feels validated because her suspicions were correct and she isn't crazy. That "elephant in the living room" finally has a name, and can be openly discussed. Partners who have been lied to for years feel some relief. This relief is immediate for some; for others it takes more time. But the reduction of anxiety and stress allows a period of time during which the couple can begin to examine the impact of the addiction on both their lives.

The primary core of healing is forgiveness, but true forgiveness can never happen unless the truth is known. When the secret or lie remains undisclosed, it festers and grows into a bigger wound. But who you tell, when you tell, what you tell, and how you tell are the keys to a successful, healing disclosure.

Forgiveness

Forgive? You probably think we are out of our minds. You may want to throw down this book at just reading that word. Your world has been turned upside down. Your heart is broken. How can we even think about talking about forgiveness at this stage of the situation? The truth is that forgiveness is for you, not the addicted person. When you get to the place you can forgive, you are no longer bound to the pain of the addiction and the addict's behavior that has been so hurtful. But forgiveness is not reconciliation. It is not condoning what has happened. It is a process that takes time, and recognizing the impact the addict's behavior has had on you is the first step.

If you want to work on your own healing then you need to know about your mate's problem. If you want your relationship to survive and grow, you have to know what has happened. Awareness of his or her difficulties gives you a better chance of identifying and dealing with your own problems.

It may be too early for you to know if you are going to stay in this relationship or not. If you are working with a therapist, she or he may have told you to take your time. Most therapists advise an addict not to make any big decisions for the first year of recovery. This is good advice and we'd recommend that to you as well. Some partners are fed up, too hurt to believe they can go on in a relationship with someone who has betrayed them so painfully. Still, if you can give yourself a chance to work on your and health and emotional healing, it will pay off no matter what you decide is best for you about the relationship.

Several things impact how well a couple does after disclosure–the type of betrayal, each person's attachment style (anxious, avoidant, or secure) and emotional competence skill level, if there have been repeated relapses, and types of unresolved issues between the couple. The commitment each person has to working on their own health and as well as the relationship health varies depending on the context of each person's life. Couples also do better when they are committed to common goals such as improving communication, co-parenting in ways that honor and protect their children, allowing each to experience feelings without returning to old ways of relating, making and accepting agreed upon restitution, and eventually moving towards rather than away from each other. This is not easy; often people are so beaten down by the unhealthy relationship that staying stuck in anger and fear seems easier than working on self-improvement or relationship skills especially forgiveness. Certainly at the point of disclosure, your mate has made decisions about moving forward, but for you, disclosure may throw you back into fear and anger and it may very difficult for you to know what you wants. Your level of emotional response is frequently a trigger for the addict, so careful planning for relapse prevention and support for you both is important.

Fortunately, with time and work towards awareness, the anger and fear do lessen, recovery gets under way and clarity about goals and decisions for the future can be made. While some level of forgiveness is essential for your peace of mind and healing, it takes time and requires much of both people in the relationship. Forgiveness may be an important part of the couple's healing work; forgiving oneself is essential for the individual to heal. Because disclosure is often the first step toward forgiveness, we want to digress here and summarize the steps to forgiveness.

According to Karl Tomm, MD of the University of Calgary there are two contrasting methods in which a person restores a sense of self-worth after being hurt. The first, often initially used by the partner, is to diminish the worth of the other through retaliation or revenge, striking out in anger and fear. The second is to enhance self-worth through competence and forgiveness (Tomm, 2002). We believe the second method is by far the better and healthier way to restore self-worth. Being able to manage your emotions is a must, but forgiveness is what enables a person to manage resentment and anger in the wake of being wronged. This is very difficult for partners, and takes time. You will have to go through a process to get to where you want or are able to forgive.

Even though we are discussing forgiveness early in the book, it does not really happen until have had a chance to understand the impact your mate's behavior has had on your life and when there has been an ample amount of evidence of changed behavior that supports his intention to change. His behavior has been a form of abuse – to you and to himself. Steps that lead to forgiveness reflect those seen in recovery from any trauma and it takes time. In her book, *The Unburdened Heart*, Mariah Burton-Nelson, a famous sports journalist, wrote about her healing journey years after having been molested by her high school coach. Burton-Nelson describes the first stage of healing as awareness that a wrong has been done and it has had a huge impact on her life. She is quick to point out that the first defense against the pain that comes with this awareness is denial. Denial is a close personal friend of every addict and most partners. The addicted person uses denial to convince himself that he won't get caught, that the behavior isn't so bad, or that this will be the last time he acts out. Likewise the partner uses denial to brush aside the evidence that something is going on, and that things will get better if she just tries harder. But without the awareness of what happened and how it affected everyone involved, it is difficult to know what impact it had on you and others and what needs to be forgiven. The disclosure process allows clarity and validation of what happened and who was responsible for what. It is through these first events of talking, listening, and validating experiences that healing can begin. Disclosure can bring an end to denial and thus a beginning to forgiveness.

In her book, *How Can I Forgive You? The Courage to Forgive, the Freedom Not To*, Janis Abrahms Spring describes four approaches to forgiveness. The first two are dysfunctional: <u>Cheap forgiveness</u> is a quick desperate attempt to preserve the relationship even if the offender ignores your pain. It is premature, superficial, and undeserved. It is offered before you process the impact of his behavior, ask anything of him, or think about what lies ahead. <u>Refusal to forgive</u> is the approach you might take when you want to punish an unremorseful mate, when you believe you can forgive only if you are ready to reconcile or have compassion for him which you do not feel, or if you believe that forgiveness is a sign of weakness.

In contrast, there are two types of forgiveness which are adaptive and useful: <u>Acceptance</u> is a healthy response to a hurt when the addict can't or won't engage in the healing process. It asks nothing of the offender, but rather is a program of self-care, part of which is to stop "giving him free rent in your head," as members of 12-step programs say. Spring calls it "clearing your head of emotional poison." Instead, you let go of revenge fantasies, ensure your emotional and physical safety, and create a relationship with the addict that satisfies your own goals, including getting along with him if that's in your best interest. You may or may not choose to have any further relationship with him. It also includes accepting that he may never change.

Finally, <u>genuine forgiveness</u> is what can happen when your mate participates in the healing process. According to Spring, genuine forgiveness must be earned, while you allow him to settle his debt. She writes, "As he works hard to earn forgiveness through genuine, generous acts of repentance and restitution, the hurt party works hard to let go of her resentments and need for retribution. If either of you fails to do the requisite work, there can be no Genuine Forgiveness."

Forgiving is healing yourself of the painful memories of the past. When you have forgiven someone, you can remember what he or she did without re-experiencing the pain. Forgiving is not forgetting or pretending that it did not happen or that the behavior wasn't such a big deal. It was and *is* a big deal for you. Forgiving is also not excusing. Excusing is appropriate when you believe the person was not to blame for the wrongdoing; you may forgive because you are ready to let go of the pain that binds you to the memory. Forgiving is also not condoning or tolerating. You can forgive him without condoning what he did. But because of what happened, you may set firmer boundaries and seek support from others as a way to protect yourself. Most likely, you will not be willing to tolerate similar actions in the future. And ultimately, you may forgive yet realize you cannot have the addict in your life.

When to Tell

Jody, married for 14 years, had watched helplessly in the past year or two as her husband Jeff became less and less engaged with her and the children. Jeff's career seemed to be sucking all his time and energy. He'd come home from work late, then spend hours at the computer at night. He told Jody he was so preoccupied because his business had sustained major financial losses and it was up to him to turn things around. Jody, who also had a busy career, tried to be supportive during what she saw as a temporary stressful time in their marriage.

One day Jeff told Jody he had signed them up for a marriage enrichment weekend. She was thrilled, telling herself that Jeff obviously still loved her and at last was ready to put some energy into their relationship. For the first time in months she felt hopeful about their future. During the two-hour drive to the retreat center where the program was to be held, Jeff told his wife that there were some things he wanted her to know. He then proceeded to reveal that he had told her hundreds of lies over an extended time period while spending many hours at the race track, drinking and gambling, more hours on the computer visiting sex sites at night when she thought he was asleep, online risks he had taken, as well as about the young woman he recently met at the dog track who had offered him a blow-job for $20 after he had won. As he drove, he began crying as he told Jody what had happened next. While he was in the restroom stall with his pants down around his ankles—never thinking he could ever do something like that – this woman stole the money he had won and the remainder of his paycheck. Jeff hoped that over the weekend Jody would have help from the other couples and the facilitators in processing the disclosure, so he told her about everything he'd done.

When the couple arrived at the retreat center, Jody was in a state of shock. The two facilitators found themselves unexpectedly faced with a woman in crisis, in need of immediate one-on-one attention. Leaving the first group session to his associate, one of the facilitators ended up spending the entire evening counseling and supporting Jody. The following morning she was able to join the group and explain what had happened.

Jeff, who'd been actively involved in addiction recovery for six months, desperately wanted his wife Jody to participate with him in recovery activities. He saw some of his program friends being supported emotionally by their spouses, speaking the language of recovery together, being able to let go of the shameful secrets they'd been keeping. But Jeff was afraid to tell Jody about his past addictive activities that he'd managed to keep secret for so long.

Finally he saw what seemed the perfect opportunity—a weekend workshop for couples recovering from addiction. Jeff had good intentions—to disclose to Jody in a setting where she would have support. But the manner in which he chose to do this was unfair to Jody and put an additional burden on the weekend facilitators, who had not planned for, and did not have the manpower for, one-on-one crisis counseling. Plus Jody was in an impossible situation—reeling from the shock and the shame and self-blame that often results from the disclosure of infidelity, she was not yet ready to have 30 other people immediately hear about her situation. Given that Jeff had the opportunity for a planned disclosure, it would have been better for him to arrange with his therapist to bring Jody into therapy, assess her emotional state, and disclose to her in therapy.

Sara and Sam had been married three years when Sam started attending Twelve-step meetings for cocaine addiction. Sara had watched in desperation as Sam sank further and further into his addiction, and was thrilled that he was finally getting help. One evening, a few weeks later, Sam called Sara right after his meeting. Sounding panicked and ashamed, he blurted out,

> "Sara, I've been at my CA meeting and the guys tell me I really need to tell you that I, ah, ah, once, when I was really out of it using crack, I hired a prostitute and had sex with her. I don't remember if I used a rubber or not, so you should go get tested for AIDS right away." He was crying now and quickly rambled, "I'm so sorry; I know you are really mad now, but please don't leave me or take Ryan. I love you both and can't live without you. I'd kill myself if you left me. Please tell me you won't leave. I'll do anything to make this up to you. Please, please, you are more important to me than anything."

Sara was stunned by what she heard. In shock she thought, "What does he mean? First the crack cocaine, now this! And an AIDS test! What is happening? What is wrong with me that he would have to have sex with a prostitute? When did this happen? My God, what am I going to do?"

The fact that Sam told her over the phone just made her confusion worse. She said, "I don't understand? What do you mean prostitute?" Then she began to scream and cry at the same time, "AIDS! How could you do this to me? Don't you love me? Was it because I wouldn't let you have anal sex with me? You told me you just had a little problem with cocaine and now you say crack! Are you really on meth? Or is it heroin? Why didn't you tell me before? Why would you lie to me like this? How could you do this to me?" As she began to sob, she slammed down the phone.

Until that phone call, Sara had had no clue that Sam was also addicted to sex and frequently sought out sexual encounters with prostitutes when he was using cocaine. During the Twelve-step meetings, his sponsor and other group members encouraged Sam to tell Sara about his sexual encounters because she may have been exposed to a sexually transmitted disease as a result of his behavior. Sam feared that disclosure would mean the loss of his marriage and his son.

On more than one occasion Sam had had sex with Sara after having had unprotected sex with a prostitute when he was high. In fact, he had admitted to his sponsor that at times he had been so unaware of reality when he was using, that it simply had not occurred to him to use a condom. His love for Sarah motivated Sam to disclose to her because he realized she needed to know that he might have exposed her to an STD, even HIV. Sam was determined to disclose but did not know how. His sponsor had suggested that Sam tell his wife in the presence of the sponsor, a therapist, or perhaps the minister from his church. But Sam, consumed with guilt and anxiety, simply sprang the news on Sara.

In the ideal world, disclosure takes place in the therapist's office, after the addict and partner have both been prepared in earlier therapy sessions to go through the initial stages of this process and have been advised how much to ask and how much to reveal. In Chapter 5, we will describe a formal disclosure from start to finish.

In reality, the first disclosure often happens precipitously when someone actually gets caught red-handed. For example, a woman may walk in on her husband when he has just snorted a line of cocaine or perhaps when he's masturbating while "chatting" with someone online or looking at pornography and demand an explanation. A man may observe his wife taking money from her mother's purse while her mother is in the restroom during dinner in a restaurant. Seeing a huge increase in the cost of automobile insurance due to a ticket for driving under the influence of alcohol may elicit questions from a partner. A man may have his credit card denied only to find when he gets home that his wife is in front of the computer, gambling online and that their bank account is overdrawn and savings depleted. A man is arrested for

IS DISCLOSURE RIGHT FOR YOU?

possession of methamphetamines while soliciting a prostitute who happens to be an undercover police officer, and he calls his wife from jail. Such situations demand immediate disclosure. Typically, the person on the spot will attempt "damage control" by revealing as little as possible, most often only what he thinks the partner already knows or is likely to find out.

Another type of precipitous disclosure occurs when the person holding the secret comes to believe he can no longer live with it, and dumps everything on an unprepared and unsuspecting partner, as happened to Jody and Sara in the vignettes above. To make matters worse, the disclosure may happen over the phone or in an email or text message rather than in person.

For example, Daniel, a physician who had had sexual relations with several patients, was admitted to a treatment center in another state. After a few days there he phoned his wife Lorelei. She reported,

> *Daniel didn't have the guts to tell me face to face, so he told me over the phone. He was safely away at the treatment center surrounded by nurturing caring professionals and fellow addicts. I was in our bedroom painting furniture, surrounded by our five small children. Laundry needed to be done; dishes from supper were waiting on me. I had to talk to him as though nothing was happening to my heart. It was horrible! I felt so alone and desperate! But what could I do?*

Lorelei continued,

> *I never would have believed for a minute he would actually have sex with anyone outside our marriage. I would actually have bet money on it. I was absolutely shocked by the seriousness and extent of his addictions and the many years he'd been lying to me. There never would have been an easy way to disclose all this stuff, but I deserved better. He described all the times he'd had sex with other people, and then said he did it because I was too tired all the time to have sex. He just went on and on. I didn't even hear half of it. I was in so much shock. I should have been given the same supportive environment as my husband, surrounded by other people in my circumstances. If I had not had those kids to take care of, I'm not sure what I would have done to myself.*

Years later, Lorelei still harbors resentment over the way this disclosure was carried out. This contaminated her ability to separate her anger at the acting out behaviors from her anger at the insensitivity of the disclosure and she admits that there is a part of her that never allows herself to trust him or be vulnerable again. Despite lots of work, she reports that his behavior has irreparably damaged the relationship.

Unexpected disclosures via letters or email are just as damaging as phone calls. Georgia, a bright young attorney, shared her story with us:

> *My husband left me a letter on what I call "the morning from hell." I was in a hurry when I left the house because I was on my way to my doctor's office to confirm a recent home pregnancy test I had taken. I just picked up that letter and stuck it in my purse and off I went, anticipating, thinking about maybe being pregnant. I forgot about the letter until I opened my purse to get in the car. Reading that letter, alone, in the car in the parking lot after leaving the doctor's office, was devastating. Here I was, just having received information that I was pregnant! This should have been the happiest day of my life—instead I was shocked beyond belief. But I had so much shame about what he said he had done, I couldn't tell anyone. I was dazed. I truly believe God drove the car the 10 miles home because I didn't even see the road. I felt suicidal—even pictured killing him and then myself. I never thought myself capable of considering those actions. I felt betrayed by the person I trusted the most. I went into shock. I was numb. I lost the baby eight weeks later and to be honest, even today I still blame him.*

Television talk and reality shows are yet another venue for inappropriate disclosures of secrets, sometimes with devastating consequences. In a highly publicized case, host Jenny Jones, in a program taped in March 1995, had a 26-year-old guest, Jonathan Schmitz, who was told only that he had a secret admirer. The secret admirer turned out to be a young gay man, Scott Amedure. The surprised Schmitz, who reportedly had a psychiatric history, was so distressed at being the public object of a homosexual crush that days later he shot Amedure dead. Schmitz was eventually sentenced to 25–50 years in prison for second-degree murder. Jenny Jones was subsequently sued successfully for her role in this murder.

The opening scene from an older movie *Hope Floats* is another good example of how not to do a disclosure. The heroine, Birdee Calvert, is invited to be a guest on a popular afternoon talk show where her best friend is going to share a "secret" with her. Birdie thinks this is just a funny gag and goes along. What her best friend tells her is that she (the best friend) is having an affair with Birdee's husband Bill. Birdee is naturally devastated as her whole life falls apart.

Electronic media has become a place for inappropriate disclosure in many ways. From sending sexually explicit photos texts or emails, to revealing information that was meant to be private, these types of disclosures often lead to disastrous endings. A tragic ending happened in September 2010, when a 19 year old student at Rutgers University, Tyler Clementi, was secretly videotaped kissing a man with a webcam set up by his roommate, Dharun Ravi while Molly Wei, a fellow dorm mate viewed the encounter in her dorm room. A couple of days later, Ravi encouraged friends and Twitter followers to watch Clementi in a second encounter with his male friend thereby disclosing (without Tyler's permission) that Tyler was gay and engaging in romantic encounters with men. Even though the viewing never occurred, Tyler was alerted of the Twitter message and the following day, Tyler tragically ended his life by jumping from the George Washington Bridge. Ravi and Wei were indicted for their roles in the webcam incident. This type of disclosure also constitutes cyberbullying. Electronic media is not the place to disclose. Information which is meant for one person and to remain private can easily be electronically shared with anyone with access to the Internet.

There is a right and a wrong way to handle revelations that result from suspicions or from incriminating evidence and disclosures that are a complete surprise to the partner. Later in this chapter we will make recommendations regarding the timing and content of these disclosures.

How Much to Tell

Unfortunately, most addicts' first attempts at disclosure come when incriminating evidence is discovered and then the addict tells only what he thinks will generate the least painful immediate consequences. Children learn early on to lie to avoid pain, and, until people get pretty healthy, they continue to repeat this behavior as adults. For addicts, it is a way of life.

In our studies of sex addicts and partners who had experienced disclosure, addicts reported that coming clean brought relief, ended denial, and proved to be the gateway to recovery for the individual and the relationship. But disclosure brings pain to the partner, and fears about loss of the relationship for both. When addicts disclose every detail, partners may have difficulty letting go.

Some addicts had revealed every single detail of their sexual acting out, and they suffered negative consequences for it. This was particularly true for addicts in early recovery. For example, Clark, 28, who'd been in recovery for 10 months when he completed the survey, wrote,

> *I feel I offered too much information. To admit I was involved with another woman was one thing, but I truly wish I had never told her who the woman was. She became obsessed with trying to find this woman and search for proof that I was still seeing her. Some people cannot handle truth and honesty as well as others. You have to know your partner and what they can handle.*

Eleven months after his disclosure, Ben, 31, related,

> *I hope it wasn't just "dumping," but I felt cleaner, relieved. But I shouldn't have shared so much, it was hurtful to her. Now it's hard for her to have so much information. The knowledge doesn't help her and seems only to cause pain as dates roll around or if we drive past a particular place. She can't stop thinking about it."*

After living with an addicted person, it is natural for a partner to easily become obsessed with his behaviors. If that obsession becomes intrusive for the partner—she literally can't stop thinking about it months or even years after the disclosure—she is having symptoms of post-traumatic stress and may need professional help. The obsession is a sign that the disclosure has gone awry.

Partners often begin by demanding complete honesty, which is a way for them to make sense of the past, to validate their suspicions and the reality they had experienced which had often been denied by the addict. Partners long to have a sense of control of the situation, to assess their risk of having been exposed to financial disaster, violence, and diseases. They want to evaluate the commitment of their partner to the future of the relationship. One partner said, "If I didn't get information, I could not trust the relationship to go forward. I needed every question answered, or I would not have been able to trust and therefore stay in the marriage. I can deal with truths, but not half-truths."

However, sometimes things get worse before they get better. Disclosure often creates more problems than the addict thinks it will. When a disclosure happens the partner may also spontaneously reveal her own set of secrets. This creates one more layer of work that has to be handled by the couple and by each individual.

Finding out that someone has been arrested and can anticipate legal consequences will affect the family for decades because of reporting requirements, probation, and loss of financial assets. In some cases the existence of another family creates ripples that members of both families will feel for years to come. One can never be 100% sure where disclosure will lead. Nonetheless, both addicts and partners have learned that honesty is the best way to find healing.

Reveal All Now, or Save the Worst for Later: The Pain of Staggered Disclosure

As the country witnessed in 1998, President Clinton's first disclosures were denials, when he repeatedly stated, "I did not have sexual relations with that woman, Ms. Lewinsky." Subsequent acknowledgments were of limited information. However, President Clinton's process of disclosure seemed to have made the situation worse for himself and his family. Despite the nation watching these staggered revelations, we have witnessed numerous public figures deny any wrong doing in the beginning, only to confess the truth later on. More recently the marriage of former California Governor Arnold Schwartzenegger ended after national news broke the story that he'd had a child with his long-term housekeeper. These are powerful demonstrations that staggered disclosure usually doesn't work for long and makes everyone angrier and less trustful. Many wives forgive their husbands after learning of an affair. But if they later learn that the husband continued to keep secrets for years while maintaining some type of relationship with an employee with whom he had daily contact, or a prostitute to whom he paid many thousands of dollars, it may become too painful to forgive.

Disclosure is painful, and often precipitates a crisis in the couple's relationship. It is hard enough for someone to admit to being a drug addict, or gambling away a family's livelihood, or having food control one's life. But disclosure is even harder for sex addicts or addicts who have both a drug and sexual addiction, often with a long list of secret sexual activities in which they have engaged. This is made even worse by an equally long list of lies that were told to cover up the activities.

When considering the consequences of the disclosure, addicts fear that the partner will leave them. Our research showed that the majority of partners do threaten to leave should they learn of an affair (in our original research, 60% of partners threatened to leave but less than one quarter of that group left). This is often the case for other types of addicts too—the partner threatens to leave if the addict doesn't stop the behavior. Female addicts in particular may fear physical or sexual violence from their partners as a response to the revelations. Both male and female addicts may worry that an angry spouse will use the information against them as a means of emotional blackmail or in a future battle for custody of the children.

It is tempting for an addict to attempt damage control by initially revealing only some of what he or she did. Often, only the least damaging information is admitted, or else only those activities that the person believes their partner already knows about. Then, at some future time, the addict discloses additional secrets, or the partner learns the whole truth independently. Unfortunately, this strategy turns out to be very short-sighted, and likely to increase the chances of an unfavorable outcome in the long run.

In our survey, 59% of addicts and 70% of partners reported that there had been more than one major disclosure. This was not always because the addict had deliberately withheld information. Some addicts did not initially remember all their actions, especially if their addictions included multiple episodes or different types of activities or drugs. In other cases, it was only after experiencing some time in recovery that the addict realized that certain behaviors were sufficiently important that they should have been divulged. The lesson here is that *disclosure is more likely to be a process than a one-time event.* Whatever the reason for the staggered disclosures, the process is particularly difficult for the person at the receiving end. It is especially destructive when the reason was a deliberate lie.

A recurrent theme among partners is the damage of staggered disclosure by the addict. When the addict claims at the time to reveal all the relevant facts but actually withheld the most difficult information for later admission, partners reported greater difficulty in restoring trust. One woman wrote:

> *There were several major disclosures over six months. I was completely devastated. He continued to disclose half truths—but only when his lies didn't make sense so that he was backed to the wall. This only increased my pain and anger and made the whole situation worse. Each new disclosure was like reliving the initial pain all over again. Part of that was not being told. I felt lied to and didn't trust any of the relationship. All I wanted was the truth. I wish the truth had been admitted all at once and not in bits and pieces.*

Another woman wrote of her feelings after her husband lost his job because of his sexual misconduct:

> *He had to tell me something because he was fired, and people in his profession are seldom fired for any reason other than gross malpractice or sexual misconduct. He told me he had sexually touched a subordinate at work. He said it was invited, which turned out not to be true. His revelations continued to dribble out over weeks as I continued to ask for information. Each new piece of information felt like a scab being ripped off.*

A similar strategy, with tragic results, was used by a physician who had sex with several patients and was asked to appear before his licensing board. Initially, he told his wife that a single patient had complained to the board; that it was all a misunderstanding. Convinced of his innocence, his wife insisted on accompanying him to the hearing to support him. It turned out that several of his victims were present and told their stories, in a very credible manner. What she heard was a litany of behaviors that shocked and stunned not only the Board, but also the local press that was in attendance. The wife said she didn't care about the other allegations, just the last one. She asked her husband if he'd had sex with that woman. At that point he felt he had to tell her the truth. He later recalled,

> I will never forget the look that came across her face. It was the look of ultimate pain that comes with betrayal, a shattered dream, a broken promise, and a broken heart. She walked out of the room and out of my life, never again to love me as a wife. I'd lost not only my career, but also my wife and daughter.

Sexually exploitative professionals and other public figures often initially try to minimize their misconduct, not only to licensing boards and assessment teams, but also to their spouses. When a wife who has publicly supported her husband because she believed in his innocence eventually learns that he continued to lie to her about the allegations after they were made public, her public humiliation and sense of betrayal are compounded, and the healing is that much more difficult.

The addict may be so frightened that what he or she has disclosed may truly be all they were capable of at the time. For example, Sam had revealed his worst behavior, but had kept to himself some other forms of sexual acting out in which he had indulged. When Sam heard that staggered disclosure is to be avoided in favor of full disclosure of all the elements of a person's sexual acting out, his eyes filled with tears and he told his therapy group,

> I was so scared to tell my wife about my voyeurism, I could barely manage to get through it. I thought I would die right there! There's no way I could possibly have told her about the other stuff. You have to realize that sometimes a partial disclosure is all you can do!

Sam's point is well taken: A partial disclosure is better than no disclosure at all, and sometimes it takes all the courage an addict has to explain to his partner *some* of what he has done. The spouse who later gets upset at hearing additional information may find it helpful to recognize that the addict may have been doing his best at the time.

One of the most important things we have learned from talking with partners of sex addicts is that staggered disclosures are very destructive to the relationship. The spouse may spend weeks or months after the initial disclosure learning to trust again, only to have the rug pulled out from beneath her or him by learning of additional secrets and lies that had not previously been revealed. In fact, often new lies had been generated to cover up the old ones, such as "I've told you everything," or "This time I'm telling you the truth." It is our belief that what is most helpful for the restoration of the relationship is for addicts initially to disclose at least the broad outlines of *all* their significant compulsive activities, rather than holding back some damaging material.

To summarize, because early on, the partner tends to want to know "everything," sometimes with negative consequences, we recommend that the partner discuss with a counselor or therapist what details are really important to know and what the likely effect will be on the partner.

Nonetheless, there are several circumstances when delayed disclosure is inevitable. This is why you need to understand that *disclosure is a process, not a one-time event.* Some situations are:

- The addict has acted out in so many different ways or with so many different people, or has told so many lies, that he or she genuinely does not recall some of them until a later time.

- The addict was in such an altered state at the time of the some of the episodes of acting out—especially when associated with drinking or drug use—that he simply does not remember particular events.

- The addict, although remembering all the details of his acting out, does not initially consider particular events or actions significant enough to bother disclosing. With increased recovery, the addict realizes the need for disclosing additional history.

- Revelation of certain actions may be so damaging to the partner or to family relations (for example, an affair with the wife's sister, purchasing and using drugs with a brother who is a minor, driving under the influence of alcohol or other drugs with children in the car), or may entail significant risk of violence to the addict (for example, a female addict married to a man who has a history of physically abusing her), that a therapist recommends not disclosing these facts initially, until the partner or family member has received counseling and preparation.

- Certain episodes of acting out occurred only *after* the initial disclosure. That is, they represented slips or relapses of the addiction. (This is the most problematic situation, in that it is likely to cause the most damage to the process of rebuilding trust.)

The take-home message is that following the first disclosure it is important to make a plan of how to manage further revelations if the addicted person later remembers more information or realizes something important has been left out.

Should I Ask for "All the Gory Details"?

In our survey, disclosure of various details often turned out to be "devastating" and "traumatic" and left recipients with unpleasant memories and associations that were difficult to ignore. Lara, who persuaded her husband to tell her "everything," regretted it:

> *I created a lot of pain for myself by asking questions about details and gathering information. I have a lot of negative memories to overcome; this ranges from songs on the radio to dates, places, and situations; there are numerous triggers.*

In later recovery, partners typically reported that they recognized that knowledge is not necessarily power, that no matter how much information they had they were still unable to control the addict. Instead, they developed guidelines for themselves about what information they wanted (typically more general information such as health risks, financial consequences affecting them, and level of commitment to recovery and the relationship) and what they did not want (such as details of what the high was like, sexual activities, locations, and numbers of partners).

Another partner spoke about the difficulty of hearing all the details.

> *I think it's best for the addict to work through it with a knowledgeable therapist, then disclose the nature of the problem and have the partner determine what level of detail they are comfortable with. For me, I didn't want any more detail, because it tormented me. Others feel they want to now everything. Not me. The bottom line I needed to know was whether he was exposing himself to disease, and then not protecting me. The actual details of who, where, and when were extremely distracting to me and caused me to lose*

ground. I'd make some progress, then think about one of those details and spiral down.

It can be very helpful for partners to have a therapist encourage them to consider carefully what information they seek rather than ask for "everything."

Private Information vs. Secret Information

In the recovering community "rigorous honesty" is virtually a dogma, and people get the idea that if the addict keeps any kind of information from his partner he is lying and thus on the verge of a relapse. Any omission becomes the catalyst for suspicion and recriminations. It is important to separate out what information is private and what is secret:

Anita had been involved with several men over the past year. Alcohol, cocaine, and having sex with men at conferences had been part of her ritual for many years. Yet when she found out she was pregnant, she knew she had to stop if she had any hope of sanity for herself or her marriage. Because her husband had had a vasectomy, she knew that the pregnancy could not possibly be his, and because of potential problems with the fetus due to her drug use, she opted to have an abortion. When she was preparing her disclosure with her therapist, she said, "I'm so confused about what to do. My peers in SLAA tell me that I am keeping secrets and harming my recovery, but I just don't think it will help our situation for me to tell him about this abortion. It was a private decision between me and my God, and not a part of our relationship. Still, I don't even know who the father was! I just don't want to screw up my recovery. Should I tell?"

In this case, Anita has done well to evaluate how it might help or further complicate the situation to tell her husband. She is correct that the decision legally is hers to make and is a private matter. If she is convinced that telling would help her stay sober, she can decide to tell information that is private. Had her husband been the father, although the decision remains hers legally, he would have had the right to know so he could at least voice his opinion, allowing him to grieve the loss and/or support her in the decision and to experience any emotions that might arise about the pregnancy and drug use. Either way, she is faced with the consequences of her decision.

How about the case of Marty, married to Suzy, who had gotten Sandy, his secretary, pregnant during a two-year affair with her. Would he be keeping a secret if he did not tell Suzy that Sandy reported having an abortion shortly after the affair ended? Is it a secret or private? Would it be different if Suzy and Marty had been trying to get pregnant for several years with no success?

In this case, Suzy had a right to know because Marty's actions could result in legal consequences (sexual harassment) since Sandy was an employee. Also, she might still be pregnant and waiting until a later date to sue him for child support and medical care. This would directly impact Suzy. To make matters worse, Sandy's best friend, who ran the local newspaper, saw Marty come out of the Motel 6 with Sandy and photographed them together. No amount of back-pedaling on Marty's part could save him from Suzy if the story about a sexual harassment suit showed up in bold print on the front page of the local paper. In order for Suzy to make decisions about staying, boundary setting, what to do if the media got involved, and what to tell the children and family members, Marty would be wise to disclose before someone else does.

It is sometimes hard to know what is private and what is a secret. What is private does not interfere with someone else's physical or emotional health or cut us off from the resources we need to solve problems. A secret prevents one person (or both) from making truly informed decisions.

Secrets sometimes become private information once they are shared with the appropriate people. So it is important to decide who else needs to know the information. It is not appropriate for the addict to tell everyone his First Step or for the spouse to tell all her friends and relatives specific information contained in a disclosure. Decide who needs to know before making the private moment between you and your spouse a public display of pain without boundaries–that is one good reason to do disclosure with a therapist who knows something about addiction and lots about couples.

Interim Disclosure

We recommend a planned, thoughtful, full disclosure as early as possible. In cases where the addict is not prepared for a full disclosure, but knows that it is quite likely you will find out about some of his addictive behavior, then an interim disclosure is in order. This means revealing the information that your mate knows you will find out anyway. You might find yourself feeling uncomfortable, frustrated, or even angry, to read that we are supporting a partial disclosure under these circumstances. Obviously, this is not the ideal. At the same time, we have repeatedly learned from partners that 1) finding out from other people before your spouse discloses to you portends a worse outcome for the relationship than when you hear it directly from him, and 2) partners benefit from having a support system (such as a therapist or someone else you trust) in place when they hear the bad news. Rather than pressing your mate for more details right now, agree to setting an appointment date to meet with your mate and his therapist for a full disclosure. Use the time between now and then to see your own therapist, make a list of the types of information you want to receive from your mate at full disclosure, and consider writing a letter describing your feelings about what's going on.

The Therapist and Secret-Keeping

How would you feel if you found out after two months of weekly couples' therapy sessions that your husband had been having an affair, and that your therapist knew about this all along but had concealed this information from you while counseling both of you about how to improve your relationship? Here is what Lorraine said about this:

> *Peter and I seemed to be growing apart. Peter had become more emotionally distant from me and the kids, spending more time at work (he said he was being given more and more assignments), and had grown more critical of me. I kept trying to improve things, but nothing seemed to help. He finally agreed to go to counseling with me. We each met with her separately once, and then together after that. The counselor told us about "I messages" and other communication techniques, and gave us various exercises. We discussed some of Peter's complaints about me and how I could change. One day Peter admitted to me that he'd been having an affair and was trying to end it, and that he had told our counselor and asked her not to tell me.*
>
> *I felt betrayed not only by Peter, but also by the counselor. How could she just sit there and talk to us about improving communication*

when we weren't addressing the really big issue? She was lying to me, just like Peter was. I was furious. How can I ever trust her to act in my interest? I told Peter I will never go back to see her again.

Therapist and clients have to decide whether or not to disclose a secret. The therapist's decision can significantly impact the effectiveness of the therapy. Some therapists continue working with the couple while holding the secret, hoping that they can still assist the couple to improve their relationship. Other therapists insist that secrets be shared and will refer you to someone else if you choose not to disclose. If you are seeking a counselor or therapist to work on relationship as well as addiction problems that include secrets, ask the therapist about his or her training and experiences. Also ask the therapist about his or her experience with addiction and the policy for insisting on disclosure if he or she sees the clients individually. How will this affect your ability to maintain recovery or trust the therapist? This should help you decide if this therapist is right for you.

The final chapter in this book is for therapists. If you have a good relationship with a therapist, you probably want to stay with him or her. You may want to share this chapter with your therapist.

The next chapter speaks more directly to the consequences of disclosure.

References

Brown, Emily M. *Patterns of Infidelity and Their Treatment.* New York: Brunner/Mazel, 1991.

Burton-Nelson, Mariah. *The Unburdened Heart.* San Francisco: Harper, 2000.

Glass, Shirley P. and Wright, T. L. "Justifications for extramarital relationships: The association between attitudes, behaviors, and gender." *The Journal of Sex Research* 29 (3): 361–387, 1992.

Herman, Judith. *Trauma and Recovery: The Aftermath of Violence-from Domestic Abuse to Political Terror.* New York: Basic Books, 1992.

Schneider, Jennifer, Corley, M. Deborah, and Irons, Richard R. "Surviving disclosure of infidelity: Results of an international survey of 164 recovering sex addicts and partners." *Sexual Addiction and Compulsivity* 5: 189–217, 1998.

Schneider, Jennifer, Richard Irons, and M. Deborah Corley. Disclosure of extramarital sexual activities by sexually exploitative professionals and other persons with addictive or compulsive sexual disorders." *Journal of Sex Education and Therapy* 24: 277-287, 1999.

Siegel, Daniel. *Emotional Intelligence*. New York: Bantam Books, 1995.

Spring, Janis Abrahms. *How Can I Forgive You? The Courage to Forgive, the Freedom Not to.* New York: HarperCollins, 2005.

Tomm, Karl, *Deconstructing Shame and Guilt; Opening Space for Forgiveness and Reconciliation.* Texas Association of Marriage and Family Therapist Annual Conference, January 2002.

Chapter Four
Consequences of Disclosure

Everyone thought that Lyndon and Loretta were the ideal couple. Married for 18 years, they were both successful health care professionals and the parents of three high achieving children. What Loretta didn't know, however, was that Lyndon had a secret life, consisting of a series of affairs with women he'd met at the hospital. Lyndon related:

> I was tired of living a double life. The lying, the sneaking around, the false reassurances to my wife whenever she questioned me,—I hated the person I had become. Finally I went to see a counselor, who recommended I join Sex Addicts Anonymous. The counselor told me I had to tell my wife if I was going to recover and that I would be wise to see a lawyer in case the situation at work created a legal problem. The guys in SAA were very supportive and that gave me some hope. However, some of the SAA members advised me to wait a year to get some clarity before disclosing to my wife, and buttressed their recommendation by quoting something from the AA Big Book supporting that position. But I loved my wife and hated that I had betrayed her. There had been so many times it had been on my lips that when my wife looked at me one day and said, "Lyndon—I'm so worried about you. You are losing weight and you are so unhappy and tormented," I broke down and told her the truth. I had not intended to, but the feeling was bigger than me.

Loretta reported:

> I felt suicidal when he told me. What would happen to our careers? What did this mean about our marriage? Would he lose his ability to prescribe or do surgery because of his actions? What would happen to our children if the media got this information? I was beside myself. I pictured killing him and then myself. I had never thought myself capable of considering those actions. If it had not been for the children, I don't know what I would have done. I felt betrayed

> by the person I trusted the most. I went into shock. I was numb. Right then and there I decided the marriage was over. I removed my wedding ring and wrote him a letter telling him I was leaving and taking the children. Then I slept in a separate room because I was afraid of what I might do since all the children were out of town.

The next day, Loretta went to see a therapist who understood addictions. The therapist advised Loretta to take some time before making any final decision about her marriage. Together they agreed to spend six months dealing with the trauma, clarifying Loretta's feelings, exploring her abandonment issues, and helping Loretta understand the extent of Lyndon's commitment to the marriage and more about how the addiction impacted her and their marriage. By the end of the six months she and Lyndon were attending a couples' support group and had decided to stay together.

Cary and Cynthia had a difficult marriage but had managed to stay together for 12 years. Part of the reason they were able to get through difficult times was because both had been in recovery from alcoholism for four years. Despite his sobriety from alcohol, Cary had not been able to manage his anger and frustrations when they fought or when he lost his job. A few years ago he had turned to Internet pornography and then arranging online for "escorts", some of whom provided additional sexual services like a prostitute. He rationalized this behavior as okay, that if Cynthia wouldn't have sex with him, he deserved to get some relief elsewhere. However, over time he had progressed from occasional use of escorts to frequent use of Internet pornography, masturbation, and arranging over the Internet to meet anonymous partners, including men, in places where he could receive oral sex. He knew he had to do something about this problem when one of the places he frequented was raided by the police just as he was driving into the parking lot. Cary's fears of giving Cynthia a sexually transmitted disease, such as herpes, HIV, or hepatitis C, led him to seek help for his addiction and ultimately to disclose to Cynthia. "I felt a great deal of shame, and was afraid that Cynthia would leave me. But I knew I had to tell her anyway."

Cynthia reported:

> I felt as if I had been deceived, betrayed, taken as a fool, victimized. I was ashamed and thought I was a "loser" for being with him

because he had done these things with men. I was so afraid and angry I was beside myself for days – screaming at him, demanding an HIV and Hep C test from my doctors and alienating those people too. Then I had to take a hard look at myself. I have to admit, I hadn't been there for him—but that isn't an excuse for his actions. But at least I hadn't been there for him because I was involved in an affair myself and now had exposed my affair partner to possible serious STDs. I had been oblivious about what was happening to him and the possible consequences my behavior might have on him. I had never stopped smoking despite saying I had on numerous occasions when he would ask me. It would have been easy for me to blame him—I did for a while. But who was I kidding! Myself! I wasn't any more sober than he was. It was so clear that I also needed more work on my recovery.

Cynthia and Cary both renewed their commitment to recovery and began marital therapy shortly after disclosure. Both agreed that disclosure opened the door to healing their marriage and got them back on track with recovery.

Mary and Bill had been married for 15 years and had two school-aged children. Mary was a very pretty, enthusiastic, and bright woman, with no college education. Yet it seemed that no matter what she embarked upon in her career, she was successful. Bill, on the other hand, had a college degree and had been in the same job, working his way up the corporate ladder at a painfully slow pace, with only one promotion during their 15 years of marriage. To others this marriage seemed perfect. However, Mary had not been content with Bill from almost the day they were married. She was disappointed that Bill was not able to progress more quickly in his job and she longed for excitement. She wanted action; she wanted to get out and do things. Bill was just boring.

Mary had begun having sexual affairs in high school, when her biology teacher had approached her during her junior year. The attention, perceived status, and risk made this liaison exciting and set a pattern for her for years to come—older men or men in positions of power and risk taking—a formula for a greater high. For all the years of their marriage Mary had had numerous affairs, all in risky situations with older or powerful men. Over time as her career grew, she had made efforts to curb her behavior because she realized the risk taking was becoming greater and greater. But her efforts were not enough.

It all came to an end when Mary and a board member of the not-for-profit agency for whom she worked were caught in the parking lot of a cheap motel engaging in oral sex on the hood of her car. Both were arrested for indecent exposure, and the call from the police station to Bill changed both his and Mary's lives. Not only was the arrest shaming and expensive, the news media made this story front page news for several days. Their children, neighbors, and relatives all were witnesses of the handcuffed professionals being shoved into the police car. Bill chose to escape with the children to his parents' home in another state, leaving Mary behind. As further revelations about Mary's past appeared in the local press, Bill decided to relocate permanently, and the couple eventually divorced. The many losses Mary experienced provided the push Mary needed to get into serious recovery, but the marriage never recovered.

Cynthia and Cary, and Loretta and Lyndon are two couples whose relationships survived and got better through disclosure. Other couples, such as Bill and Mary, did not reunite, but despite their divorce Mary was glad the disclosure forced her to get help and into recovery. No matter what the reason for the disclosure, it is a process rather than a one-time event. The first step is to identify and face the fears that come with disclosure.

Preparing to Manage Emotions

Emotions run rampant before, during, and after a disclosure. It is common for partners to report combinations of feelings, ranging from relief and hope to rage and despair. Of course an addict who is planning a formal disclosure has been planning and rehearsing what he will say in his head or with his sponsor, a friend, or therapist. Prior to the disclosure he feels nervousness, fear, anxiety. Most addicts hope that telling will in some way help, but fear a whole host of losses and do not want to suffer the consequences.

Joe, a 43-year-old electrician and father of two children, recalled:

> *I had so much shame; I did not know how I was going to get through it. My self-worth had hit bottom and I felt like a worthless piece of*

shit. I was so depressed; often suicidal, but did not even have the guts to do that. I was scared she would never believe me again or worse, yet, she would leave and take the kids. I couldn't blame her if she did. I felt like such a failure, like scum, horrified that I hurt her so much.

No matter what the circumstances, you will have a variety of emotions throughout the disclosure process and in the aftermath when you are trying to get a handle on what to do next. Most likely the addict has had lots of time in the past days or weeks to think about his actions and how to disclose to you, and may well be in control of his emotions, while you may be reeling with shock or feeling anger, fear and self-blame. You can anticipate a rocky road ahead for the near future, and your reactions are very normal. What you need next is some support. If you are the recipient of a planned disclosure, then presumably the therapist has thought in advance about providing you with some support. Otherwise, this is the time to talk to a trusted friend or family member or your own therapist. In Chapter Nine we will talk about the need to choose an appropriate confidante. Although disclosure can be initially devastating to the partner, it does have positive outcomes in the long run, and we will discuss these below.

Positive Outcomes of Disclosure

If disclosure had only the negative consequences reported later in this chapter, it is unlikely that addicts, partners, and couples who have been through this experience would recommend disclosure to others. In our survey we asked addicts and partners if they thought disclosure was the right thing to do. We asked them to think both retrospectively about how they felt at the time of the disclosure and how they felt about it when they completed the survey, which was weeks to years afterwards. Thinking back to the time of the disclosure, over 80 percent of the partners and more than 60 percent of the addicts reported they felt at the time that it was the right thing to do. The next statistic is even more impressive. At the time of the survey, that number had risen significantly. *Of the partners, 93 percent felt it had been the right thing to do. And a whopping 96 percent of the addicts felt disclosure was the right thing to do!* Despite all the pain and loss, enough good had to come out of the process for people to feel so strongly that it was the right thing to do and the majority said they would recommend disclosure to other couples.

Both partners and addicts experience significant positive aspects of disclosure. For both partners, these include:

- Honesty
- End to denial
- Hope for the future of the relationship
- A chance for the partner to get to know the addict better
- A new start for the addict, whether in the same relationship or not.

Additionally for partners, other significant positive outcomes from the disclosure include:

- Clarity about the situation
- Validation that they are not crazy
- Hope for the future of the relationship
- Finally having the information necessary to decide about one's future.

Jessica, who had been through a painful disclosure, reflected,

The disclosure hurt, was more traumatic than I thought possible, and at the same time the information was sort of a relief because now I knew I wasn't going crazy. My instincts were accurate, he had lied for years. For about two years I had suspected something. I can now understand the past, it helped me understand why he acted the way he did. I felt relieved to finally know the truth. Now I could make choices based on the truth, not some lies.

Misty, a 45-year old accountant who'd been married for 23 years, was one of many women whose husbands had covered up their behavior by casting doubts on their wives' emotional state, teling her she was imagining things. Despite her pain, Misty felt that the disclosure was very helpful to her:

I needed to know what kind of risks I was taking. Knowing he could relapse with men and prostitutes let me know how to protect myself

from STDs. I also had suspicions about when he was active in his addiction in the past. By finding out that I was accurate in my hunches about his behavior, I learned I can trust myself and I'm not crazy, or at least I wasn't making things up or overly suspicious. It started us off on a footing of greater honesty.

Echoing a common theme reported by partners, Lydia, aged 38 recalled,

The disclosure let me know he cared about me enough to share that difficult information. It meant he loved me enough to be honest with me. I saw it as an opportunity to seek help. This might be a beginning.

In our study, here is what addicts reported as positive aspects of disclosure:

Sydney, writing two years after his original disclosure, said,

In some ways the disclosure was selfish. I couldn't stand the pain of the double life. This is who I really am. I had been so manipulative she had no idea the depth of my emptiness or my compulsive use of prescription drugs, for so many years, working at a job that used me, trying to be the somebody I wasn't, trying to fill that void. Disclosure was proof that I had a real chance to stop my out-of-control behavior because I could not continue on the course my life was taking if I wanted to live.

According to Eldon, another addict,

I was so tired. Porn on the Internet owned me. I found myself in such physical and emotional pain, having realized I had snuck out of bed so many nights to spend most of the night looking for that never obtainable high again, masturbating until I was numb, back hurting, dehydrated and realizing that I had to try to sleep a half hour and get up for work. I did not have to keep on living with this secret, feeling so shitty all the time – I had to get some help. Though I had admitted to some use before, the full disclosure and my honesty about how I was really feeling, I found out my partner really loved me and was willing to go to therapy with me and help me solve my problems with this addiction.

Peter recognized,

It meant that I had to admit to myself and my wife that I was gay. My marriage of 27 years ended, but it was not really an adverse consequence. It was the right thing for both of us. We survived it and remained friends.

Adverse Consequences of the Disclosure for the Partner

Although the above responses reflect the feelings of hope, the relief for partners to finally gain clarity about the past, and the recognition by some addicts that living a double life was more destructive than opening up, we will not gloss over the intense feelings people have during this process. Initially after disclosure, adverse consequences for both addicts and partners that usually disappear after a period of time include sleep loss and obsessive thinking, loss of appetite, stomach pain, diarrhea, sometimes vomiting, and weight loss. Worry and lack of concentration interfere with work performance and day-to-day tasks. It is as though someone close to you died and the grief process crashes over you like a tidal wave. Not being able to focus makes everything harder. Depression makes decision-making difficult; making mistakes is common. Car accidents are commonly reported.

Just like the majority of addicts, partners also recommended disclosure. Yet, partners also reported that each went through what seemed like the worst nightmare of their lives. Recent studies have reported symptoms that reflect the trauma most partners suffer when disclosure, especially disclosure when they had been told in the past that nothing was wrong or received only a partial disclosure

Mary, 42, had a traumatic reaction:

I felt like I'd been stabbed right through the heart; the pain took my breath away. I didn't feel that I could breathe or would live. I felt frozen in time; I had overwhelming terror about what would happen next. I was paranoid about everything and had no faith in my ability to make decisions. I couldn't sleep, couldn't concentrate, wasn't able to take care of my kids or anything else – I just fell apart for a while.

For many partners, the impact of the addiction which comes to light through the disclosure represents an attachment injury, wherein the relationship becomes a source of danger instead of a safe haven in times of emotional distress. When an attachment bond is violated or broken, the person often suffers pain that we call *relational trauma.* As in any other trauma, initially the partner may respond in one of two ways –she will either make a valiant attempt to get the spouse to reconnect or will build an emotional wall shutting out the addict, not wanting to ever allow herself to be vulnerable again.

Receiving addiction information is especially a traumatic experience for the partner. Knowing you have been lied to is bound to cause pain. When the secret activities have been sexual, the pain and the sense of betrayal are more acute. Partners often seriously consider the likelihood that the relationship will not survive the truth about the addict's behavior. Adding insult to injury, there are cases in which an arrest has been made, financial security lost, or a life-threatening or incurable disease may have been transmitted. Sometimes addicts have another totally separate life, with another family, children who see the addict as a father and for whom the addict has financial responsibility. If there are legal consequences with law enforcement or the Internal Revenue Service, or if the addict has lost his or her job, both you and your mate are plunged further into fear.

The anger or resentment you may feel because of this threat is sometimes insurmountable. In addition, the core fear of abandonment that many partners of addicts feel is often triggered by the disclosure. You can expect that this will be a traumatic experience for you, that the family will change, and that the consequences of your mate's behaviors may last for years.

The feelings may be so intense you think your head or heart will explode. There is a combination of anger, grief, confusion, pain, fear, and sometimes revulsion. The obsession that invaded your brain takes a new turn. Before, you might have suspected something, but now the obsession turns to worrying about how you missed it, what is wrong with you that this happened, and you worry about what will happen in the future. Theresa, a 43-year-old cashier and mother of three, reported,

> *I couldn't believe what I was hearing. This was the man that I thought I could trust. This was my life, blowing up in front of me. I had never doubted myself any more than I did at that moment. What was*

wrong with me that something like this could happen? And how did I miss something this big? Then afterward, I lost my relationship with my family when they found out. I would have flashbacks of him telling and I couldn't stop the hurt, the loneliness, the isolation I felt. I couldn't tell anyone for the longest time. I couldn't sleep. I felt so old and tired, worn out. Not only couldn't I trust him with drugs and alcohol and money, now if he used—it meant he would be using crack in some hotel, wearing my clothes, and masturbating to some porn on the cable TV. God . . . How the hell do you get beyond that?

Among the adverse consequences that can be expected as a result of disclosure are:

- A worsening of the couple relationship
- Depression and even suicidal thoughts
- Attempts to compensate for the pain with acting-out behaviors such as over or under eating, alcohol and other drug use and even sex
- Loss of self-esteem
- Decreased ability to concentrate or to function at work
- Feelings of shame and guilt
- Distrust of everyone
- Anger and rage
- Fear of abandonment
- Physical illness
- Lack of sexual desire

Some partners reported becoming depressed, distracted, and even suicidal. According to Phil, whose partner had starting having sex with other men when using crystal methamphetamine, supposedly to lose weight, "I couldn't concentrate. I got into two car accidents and did things like putting milk in the cupboard and cereal in the refrigerator. I was afraid I would drive off a particular bridge and was afraid I would hurt myself with a kitchen knife."

CONSEQUENCES OF DISCLOSURE

Millie's husband told her a project at work required him to stay late for several months. In reality, he was spending hours every evening in cybersex activities in his office. He exchanged and downloaded S & M pornographic pictures on his work computer, engaged in real-time online sex involving bondage and domination, and occasionally had real-life sexual assignations with women he'd "met" online. After learning of her husband's double life, Millie said,

> *I felt total distrust in myself, in him, in the relationship. I felt betrayed, confused, afraid, stunned that the person I loved and trusted most in the world had lied about who he was, and that I had lived through some vast and sinister cover-up.*

Other partners described their insecurity and loss of self-esteem at feeling unable to compete with sexual partners, the power of drugs, or the seduction of gambling or high-risk spending. Some partners have to have time away to think and let the anger subside. Sometimes there is a feeling of being suffocated by the presence of the addict.

Marie, whose husband had spent hundreds of hours on the Internet experimenting with various illegal sexual practices, including viewing teen pornography and engaging in sex with minors, explained, "I was so devastated and repulsed by him. I didn't want him to touch me; I hated him and wanted him to leave. I loathed him and wanted him dead. The betrayal on all levels was just more than I could take."

Samantha's spouse of 20 years revealed a long history of unprotected sex with prostitutes while using cocaine. For years they had struggled to make ends meet. Time and time again she had had to explain to her children that there was no money for new school clothes or toys at Christmas. This information brought back all the sadness from those times of deprivation,

> *I'd been victimized and I took it personally. He could have killed me with HIV. It was like someone had taken a shotgun and blasted me all over, the pain was unbearable and I couldn't stand to be around him. I was embarrassed and humiliated. I couldn't bear to think what to tell the kids—how do I explain to them that they mean so little to their father that he would spend money we did not have just to please himself. I hate him and myself for being with him.*

Constant confusion is common for the partner who can't decide if she wants him there or not:

> I didn't trust him and I couldn't find the pride that I once felt. I'd get reminded of something, some lie he had told and the feelings would start all over again. I'd want him out of my sight. 'Just get out, get out!' I'd yell. Sometimes I thought I just want to cut my losses and give up on him, get on with my life. Then he would be gone a while and we'd go out and before I knew it he was back in my house again.

Some couples experience several separations and reconciliations:

> Sometimes I thought I was going crazy. He would move out for three or four months and then back in to figure out what HE wanted. I suffered abandonment each time and waited for him to make up his mind. Neither of us had enough recovery to deal with it.

Some partners use alcohol and other drugs to "soften the blow." This can be a time of high risk for relapse by partners who are also addicts. Some partners have more sex with the addict because of their fear of losing him or to prove they can keep up. Others get involved in a revenge affair, sometimes disclosing and other times keeping their own secret. Too often partners report that they end up in a liaison with someone they have turned to for help such as a work colleague, a friend of the addict, and in some cases even the attorney, physician, or therapist from whom they are seeking professional services. A rebound affair was reported by several partners. After the first rush of intensity, this did not prove to be a constructive solution to the couple's problems: It complicated their efforts to put the relationship back together, caused additional distrust, and often resulted in depression for one or both partners.

Friends frequently choose sides and, depending on how much is disclosed to them, can share information that should be private with people who do not need to know. Family members often side with the partner and are incensed when she doesn't leave, so they sever the relationship. This is yet another disruption and often very painful for the partner and the children. If acting out behaviors are illegal, sometimes children are removed from the home—an extremely traumatizing event for children which compounds the pain of the betrayal.

The understanding that learning about infidelity constitutes a traumatic experience for the partner is receiving increasing attention from therapists who treat partners of sex addicts. But this approach has been used for years by various knowledgeable therapists. For example, here's what Shirley Glass wrote in 2003 in *NOT Just Friends*:

> *The revelation of infidelity is a traumatic event for the betrayed partner. Understanding it as traumatic has important implications for healing people who have just found out about a partner's affair may react as if they have been viciously attacked. Where they formerly felt safe, they now feel threatened. In an instant, the betrayed spouse's assumptions about the world have been shattered. Commonly, betrayed spouses become obsessed with the details of the affair, have trouble eating and sleeping and feel powerless to control their emotions, especially anxiety ad grief, which can be overwhelming. . . . Because betrayal is so traumatic and recovery takes time, I use an interpersonal trauma recovery plan that parallels the ones recommended for victims of natural disasters, war, accidents, and violence (pages 9-10).*

Adverse Consequences for the Addict

Addicts who reveal their secret life to their partners can expect to experience some of the following adverse consequences:

- Worsening of the couple relationship
- Guilt and shame
- Anger and sometimes rage from the partner
- Loss of trust by the partner
- Limiting access to the children
- Cutting off of the sexual relationship
- Damage to other relationships, such as with children or friends
- Legal consequences
- Loss of job

Steven, 36, who had been in recovery from nicotine, alcohol, and benzodiazepines for five years, relapsed when a friend showed him how to get around the filter on his computer and view the extremes that existed in pornography websites. Just when he thought it couldn't get better, his friend showed him how to engage in interactive sexual sites using his webcam. Steven was immediately drawn to the excitement of actually seeing someone do what he commanded. Before long he found himself smoking again at the computer. After several offline hookups, during which he resumed drinking, he returned to AA where his old sponsor told him he needed to tell. But the disclosure brought consequences Steven had not expected:

> *There were fights before but now she had the ammunition she needed to keep me in line. She didn't trust me anymore. The doubt about what I might have done or might do in the future was debilitating— she tried to control my behavior to prevent my acting out. She was continually accusing me of affairs, acting out – even accused me of using crystal meth even though I hadn't gone that far. It was a nightmare for her and for me.*

After admitting her affairs to her husband, 37-year old Suzy told us,

> *My husband wanted to 'reclaim' me sexually. I felt so guilty that I let him consume me sexually for weeks. Then I became disgusted and started shutting him out. He then became vigilant about my behavior, thoughts, and actions for several months. He started to judge me and try to manage my program. Now when he is feeling insecure or mad, he brings up my history and throws up certain situations or individuals to me. I don't know what to say; I just feel worse, guiltier.*

Other addicts complained that their partner was monitoring their every movement, or constantly reminding them of past transgressions, or withholding sex as punishment or because the partner did not feel safe.

It is not uncommon for an addict to lose his or her job as a result of acting out in the work site or as a result of public exposure of some illegal acting out behavior. Sometimes illegal behaviors lead to formal charges against the addict, huge legal costs, and even incarceration.

The financial consequences can also be immense. Therapy and treatment are expensive; legal costs are even more costly. If job loss is a consequence, then financial problems are even greater. Often acting out has been associated with spending money—on pornography, prostitutes, gifts, drugs, and alcohol. Some addicts have led such a double life that they have another household set up; some even have other children to support. But the truth of the matter is, *even without disclosure most addicts experience these consequences.* Addicts need to realize that *the worst consequences are a result of the experience, not the disclosure.*

Do Partners Leave As Result of Disclosure?

Most addicted persons worry that they will lose the relationship, and the fear that the partner will leave is a huge deterrent to disclosure by the addict. But do partners actually leave? Threats to leave are a common, easily understood reaction to the shock of learning that your mate has betrayed you with another person. About 70 percent of partners have some suspicions about the addict's behavior long before their mate admits the secrets. Some partners confront their significant other; others keep quiet either because the addict has said it was their imagination, or they fear the consequences of saying anything. They may want to avoid confrontation at all costs, or else because they feel everything is their fault. Norma reported,

> *I had a few suspicions, just a feeling. I tried to ignore it and look at the good in our relationship. Finally I brought my feelings to him and said I felt suspicious. I proceeded to tell him that it must be just me, that I might need to get help. He let me take all the guilt and blame on myself, though he was the one using.*

Those who do confront are sometimes met with active resistance. Sylvia, now divorced, wrote,

> *I was very naive and out of touch. A part of me knew that he was doing weird stuff and he even told me in subtle ways about it, but I wanted to minimize it all. When I told him about my fears, he would get extremely violent and throw things and break things and refuse to talk to me.*

Jeremy related,

> *When I told Betty about my suspicions, she threw a fit. She accused me of not trusting her, said that if I wasn't satisfied I was free to move out, and stormed out of the house, leaving me with the*

four kids. She didn't return until next morning. I didn't say a word about it after that.

Lorelei, the wife of a physician mentioned in Chapter 3 who had multiple affairs, said,

I had suspicions because he would not answer his cell phone and would come home late, sometimes reeking of cigarette smoke and alcohol. He would blatantly deny doing anything wrong. He'd be insulted that I questioned him and would often manipulate the scene and argue that I was pathetic and paranoid. Sometimes I would back down and actually apologize for accusing him. Then I would feel a terrible guilt.

Confrontation and denial are a recurrent theme in the relationships of addicts and their partners. This results in a pattern of dishonesty by the addict and distrust by the partner, which subsequently makes it difficult for the couple to restore trust in their relationship.

In many cases, suspicions about secret activities result in threats to leave even before any disclosure is made. About 40 percent of partners make such threats, which understandably gives pause to men and women who are considering disclosing their secrets.

Receiving a disclosure can be painful, terrifying, hurtful, anger-provoking, and possibly the worst thing a person has ever experienced. Our research indicated what we have seen clinically for years: For some, the information is just too much to take. The partner feels wounded and has no interest in trying further, leaves or demands the addict leave and takes steps to obtain a divorce.

Although some partners immediately close ranks with the addict and promise support, a majority (60 percent in our study) threaten to leave or to end the marriage or committed relationship. However, a large majority of partners (72 percent in our study) do not act on this threat. Among those who do separate, about half eventually reunite. For those who seek separation first, this seems to allow enough distance for both the addict and partner to seek support and help. Addicts new to recovery require intense focus on their recovery programs; partners have equally difficult times healing from the trauma of the addict's behavior and need time and space to practice self-care. While not all separations are temporary, even couples who end their relationship often remain friendly and co-parent in healthier ways. So separation initially isn't all bad.

Partners are just as likely as addicts to come from dysfunctional families in which their own childhood needs for nurturing were not met. You may believe that love must be earned by giving. You may have been initially attracted to the addict because this was a person who seemed to carry childhood wounds, who needed to be helped, or whose family background was familiar.

Many partners of addicts have childhood wounds that result in a great fear of abandonment. Life without the addict may seem like a fate worse than death. Although they may threaten to leave as a result of receiving a painful disclosure, some partners are unable to take effective action because of their own fears. They may conclude that living with the pain is better than living alone, or may decide to give the addict "another chance." Some rationalize their lack of action; others simply postpone making a real decision. Still others have to consider the consequences of leaving on their children and financial situation, so stay almost out of default. This rarely turns out to be a good thing for anyone if the partner is not also able to get support and help.

Threats Before and After Disclosure

Partners who threaten to leave when they only suspect infidelity might be expected to threaten to leave once their suspicions are confirmed. Interestingly, however, about a quarter of partners who threaten to leave on the basis of suspicions *before* disclosure do not make the same threat following disclosure. The reasons given by two women were:

> *I was so happy he was finally in recovery that I felt we could make it as a couple.*

> *I stayed because of the serious level of his addictions—I believe he is so sick. I could not think of breaking up our relationship as long as he is 100 percent committed to a serious recovery program.*

Although some partners threaten to leave, often they will demand the addict get therapy and attend Twelve-step meetings. Many times during the process, the therapist will invite the partner to a few sessions or will refer the addict and partner to another therapist for couple's therapy. This can represent an opportunity for the couple to learn new ways of relating and help them get back on track to a happier life.

Partners' Reactions to Disclosure of Relapse

Relapse unfortunately is a frequent part of all addictive disorders. We recently studied a group of partners who had experienced one or more disclosure of relapse by their sexually addicted mate. Unlike the initial disclosure of the addiction, which had been a surprise, most partners suspected that the mate had relapsed before his or her disclosure. It seems that having become much more knowledgeable about sex addiction, partners were able to detect the signs. It is a sign of appropriate self-care that partners are tuned into their spouse's behavior. Most of the relapses involved the use of the internet, either to view pornography or to engage in other online sexual behaviors.

It is interesting that partners' decision making about staying or leaving is somewhat different after disclosure of relapse than after the initial disclosure of the addiction. After the initial relapse, partners tend to react in a black-and-white manner, threatening to leave although many reconsider, at times after a separation. They are understandably focused on the addict's acting-out behaviors and the pain it has caused them. After disclosure of relapse, however, many partners decide on the basis of two other factors – the addict's motivation to change and his or her honesty in the relationship. Several partners said that that their shared history and their positive relationship would make it worth staying as long as the mate was honest to them and committed to recovery. Partners are also more aware that addicts are at significant risk of relapse and many are willing to consider that addiction recovery can be a series of steps and may expect "progress, not perfection." Addicts are understandably reluctant to disclose a relapse for fear that this time the partner really *will* leave them. Our research showed that when partners actually discovered the relapse on their own, the outcome was likely to be worse than if they learned about the relapse from the addict. Lying and the resultant inability to trust the mate were commonly reported reasons that would make partners consider leaving.

Conclusions

Disclosure of secrets, especially painful secrets involving sexual activity with others, usually precipitates a crisis in the couple's relationship and an initial worsening of the relationship. Both partners and addicts experience a series of adverse consequences. In addition to possible legal, health, and job consequences, the addict typically feels guilt and shame, anger at the partner, resentment that the partner no longer trusts the addict and may now keep him (or her) on a short leash. The addict often has to go through a period where the partner is not interested in a sexual relationship.

Partners who have been on the receiving end of a disclosure typically experience depression and even suicidal thoughts, fear of abandonment, loss of self-esteem, decreased ability to concentrate or to function at work, distrust of the addict and perhaps of everyone, anger, lack of sexual desire, physical illness, and at times, attempts to compensate for the pain with acting-out behaviors such as misuse of food, drug use, and sex. As part of their distress and anger, many partners react to the disclosure by threatening to leave. Fear of this possibility can prevent addicts from revealing secrets, even if they wish to unburden themselves as part of their own recovery process.

The good news, as we learned from many couples that have been through this process, is that most people who threaten to leave don't do so. Even when the couple does separate, the chances are good that they will reunite if each is committed to their individual recovery from their addiction and trauma. Disclosure can lay the groundwork for a new relationship, based on honesty and greater intimacy.

In later chapters we will describe how counselors can facilitate disclosure, what couples who have been through the process recommend to other couples, how much to reveal and when, and what tools of recovery are helpful for rebuilding trust and restoring the relationship. To prepare, we'd like to ask you to think about the following questions as they apply to your own life:

- What do you fear the most about being disclosed to?
- What sources of strength do you have to get you through this time?

- Who can you call to support you during this time?
- What skills do you need to improve to handle your reaction to the disclosure?

The next chapter gives steps for a formal disclosure.

References

Corley, M. Deborah & Schneider, Jennifer P. Partner reactions to disclosure of relapse by self-identified sexual addicts. *Sexual Addiction and Compulsivity*, 2012

Glass, Shirley. *NOT Just Friends*. The Free Press, New York, NY, 2003

Schneider, J.P., Corley, M.D., and Irons, R.R. Surviving disclosure of infidelity: Results of an international survey of 164 recovering sex addicts and their partners. *Sexual Addiction and Compulsivity* 5: 189–217, 1998.

Chapter Five

The Formal Disclosure: How to Do It Right

Most initial disclosures are not planned. They are prompted either by external events such as a partner's suspicions or discovery, or by being confronted by an employer, neighbor, or the police because of some illegal behavior; or else by intense internal emotions that can no longer be tolerated. Depending on the specific circumstances, the addict's personality, his current emotional state, and his fears of the outcome, he may disgorge the entire story, replete with details; alternatively, he may attempt damage control by revealing as little as possible. The partner may be shocked by the completely unexpected revelations, or she might have been already suspicious and relieved in some way to be actually getting some information.

Take the story of Jada and Jordan. When they met as college seniors, Jada was a serious and introverted young woman who was very attracted to Jordan, who loved adventure and travel and whose childhood dream was being a pilot. Twenty years later, now parents of a daughter, Jada had a rewarding career in information technology and Jason was enjoying flying for a major airline. Both were doing exactly what they loved to do professionally. With time, however, Jada noticed that Jordan's *joie de vivre* seemed to have diminished somewhat, that he seemed distracted and took on more responsibilities and more flights for the airlines. Jada's response was to assume more home responsibilities, while trying to make their time together more enjoyable for Jordan by planning more outings for them and even organizing social activities at their home although she preferred their quiet time. Jordan faithfully phoned or texted Jada when he was out of town, brought her gifts from foreign countries, and told her he loved her. She knew he was a fun-loving guy, and believed he was doing his best to fulfill his role as a husband despite the frequent absences that his job required.

What Jada didn't know was that Jason had had a secret life for several years. All she knew was that for the past year Jason appeared increasingly preoccupied so that at times she felt he wasn't really listening to what she was telling him. One evening, however, over dinner in a nice restaurant, surrounded by many people and after drinking four martinis to bolster his courage, Jordan suddenly announced to Jada that he had something really bad to tell her. He had been home sick for a week, so she wondered whether he had some serious health condition. Alarmed, she put her wine glass down and stared at him with tears in her eyes. Jordan said,

> Jada, I have been really horrible. Three years ago at my 25th high school reunion I ran into an old girlfriend who really came on to me. She made me feel young again, and we ended up in bed. We continued to see each other all this time, but it is over now. However, there are complications. I'm in a big mess at present. The fact is, I haven't been sick, just avoiding telling you that I got suspended from work last week because she and I were caught with her giving me oral sex in a car at the airport—all of the crew knows. She wanted me to leave you and marry her. Really she trapped me with sex and now she is claiming she is pregnant and she says I am the father. I have talked to our attorney and he is advising me to go to a treatment center for a month, thinking that I drank so much during this affair that I might have a drinking problem that impaired my thinking. Anyway, I have to leave tomorrow morning. I knew I had to tell you before I left. I love you, not her and I am sorry for messing up our lives.

Jada was so shocked by Jordan's words that she uncharacteristically threw her wine on him and stormed out of the restaurant, after telling him he need not come home. She felt outrage and disbelief that he had been lying to her and cheating on her for years and that she hadn't been aware of it. She wondered if there was something wrong with her that she had believed him. She was angry that she had worked so hard to make his life good while in fact his focus had been elsewhere. She wanted nothing more to do with him, while at the same time she felt grief at the thought that their marriage was over. She wondered how she could explain all this to their teenage children. She refused to talk to Jordan during the first three weeks he was in treatment. It was their attorney who helped her see that avoiding him and the situation wouldn't change things. She agreed to talk to him and to attend the therapy at the treatment center that was highly recommended for family members during the fourth week of an addict's treatment.

In treatment, Jordan followed the steps outlined in this chapter to present a formal disclosure to Jada. (See Jordan's second disclosure in the box on page 72). The disclosure was initially devastating for her. She learned that the affair with Deondra was not, as she had assumed, a unique experience for Jordan, but that he had had affairs throughout their marriage, while risking her health by having unprotected sex. Jada was able to process the disclosure with therapists at the treatment center as well as with Jordan. She felt a huge loss at the thought that the life she thought they had shared was actually very different from the reality; she realized she had to reframe their entire marriage history. She recognized that for years much had been going on in her life and marriage that she had not paid attention to.

When she returned from the family session, Jada joined a support group for partners of sex addicts and began her own therapy. It was extremely difficult for her for the first several months of her therapy. Upon Jordan's return, they both attended individual and couple's therapy. Realizing that other couples also faced similar tragic circumstances, they found the strength and support to sustain them during the challenging months to resolve the problems resulting from Jordan's actions. Jada recognized that as painful as Jordan's disclosures were to her, they were also difficult for him, and the fact that he did disclose extensively to her indicated that he wanted things to work out for them and was willing to do what it takes. His ongoing honesty, in small as well as big matters (a real contrast from his previous pattern of lying) gradually helped Jada to begin to trust him again, a process that took a couple of years, as it does for many couples.

Jordan and Jada have now been married almost 25 years. Their daughter has completed school and is training to be a pilot herself, while their son became a computer programmer. They provide financial support for the child born to Jordan and Deondra and enjoy having him as part of their family during various holidays and each summer. They were lucky, but there were many consequences. Jordan lost his job with the airline. He was able to find a job as a private pilot of a person in recovery, but not before Jada's parents found out and encouraged her to leave him. Their daughter struggled with school and emotional distress for several months. Jada was plagued with flashbacks and weeks of insomnia. Luckily, they had the resources for all who were involved to get therapy. Both agreed that the second disclosure and the therapy everyone got helped them start from an honest place in their marriage. With that beginning, lots of faith in a Higher Power, and support from the friends they finally disclosed to, it was possible to start a new way of living.

Jordan's Second Disclosure

(This letter was read during a family session while Jordan was in treatment.)

Dear Jada,

I know I have disclosed some of the "facts" to you but I did not do a very good job. I am sorry about the way I told you those things. Once again, I was selfish and did not consider the impact on you. Now, I want you to know the truth about everything and am willing to answer any questions you have now or in the future.

First, I tell you these things with a heavy heart. I know you always thought we had a good marriage. What happened and is happening is not fair to you or our daughter. What I did was wrong and I am sorry you are suffering the consequences for what I did. It isn't fair and I can't expect you to forgive me.

I want you to know, you did not do anything to cause what has happened. I made the choices I made because of the way I was thinking. That is not your fault; it is mine. You are a good woman, a good wife, and a good mother. I do not blame you or anyone else for what has happened. I am responsible. Deondra did not trick me, I did what I did because I was selfish and thought the rules did not apply to me. I was wrong.

I have learned lots about myself since I came to treatment. One of the things is that I am a liar. I have lied to boost myself up. I did not want to admit and sure did not want anyone, especially you, to know how insecure I felt. I have been a liar for so long; I don't know when I started and haven't always known when I was telling a lie. It is important that you know I do know now and am remembering how much I lied to you. I lied about how I was feeling, I lied about money, where I was, the people I was with. I told lies that suggested that you were at fault, or stupid for suspecting me. Remember when you asked me about the perfume you smelled on my uniform so often and I said you were paranoid, that it was just perfume from sitting next to a flight attendant on the bus. I was wrong to have lied and I am sorry for all the times I made you question yourself. It must have made you feel crazy at times. You were not crazy or stupid or foolish then and you are not now.

You were right to suspect me. I have had several affairs since we have been married. As well as I can remember, the affairs started after I got that "ass-chewing" from one of the dads at Shari's soccer game. I felt like everyone on that field thought I was a fool and just couldn't get it out of my mind. Instead of going to you to talk about it, I picked up a flight attendant who had been telling me all about her marital problems for weeks. Most of the women have been flight attendants. I have not been with anyone that you are friends with or that you know other than Deondra and I think you only met her briefly at the class reunion. That is where I hooked up with her and started seeing her shortly thereafter.

I have spent thousands of dollars that should have gone for things for you and the kids. I have put my career in jeopardy and by doing so have put your future and that of our children in jeopardy. I was horrible to do so and I am sorry. Our attorney tells me my supervisor is seeing my time in treatment as favorable, but I will not know the outcome of the suspension until I am finished with treatment. I am sorry for placing you in this position. I know you must be worried about what to do next.

The most difficult thing for me to admit is that I have had unprotected sex with many of these women. Not only have I exposed you to sexually transmitted diseases, there is a baby on the way who will be my financial responsibility. I have had an HIV test and it has come back negative, but if you have not had one yet, you should.

> I would not blame you if you wanted a divorce. I do not want that, but I would understand how you may feel like you can never trust me again.
>
> I hope my honesty here and my behaviors from this point forward will help you see that I am serious about our marriage. I want to be your best friend. I know you thought we were, but I wasn't. I understand that honesty is the major quality of a best friend. That is where I have to start—not just for you and our marriage, but for my own sanity.
>
> I can't expect you to forgive me but I am hoping that you will give me a chance to re-establish a new, healthier relationship with you. I love you and the kids with all my heart.

Not all disclosures end happily, but as we've said before, the majority of couples interviewed agreed they were glad they disclosed. This was true even if the relationship ended. Ideally, disclosure allows people to make decisions based on accurate information instead of lies.

It is important to point out that disclosures do change everything and in the beginning change creates stress. The family dynamics change. Sometimes, like in Jordan and Jada's case, another child is involved and therefore another family. Careers are involved. Finances are affected. People at work or in the neighborhood often find out and unimagined consequences can result. So be prepared for changes.

How and What to Tell

In Chapter 3 we discussed the steps to forgiveness, and explained that forgiveness is primarily for *you*, for your peace of mind, not for the person who hurt you. Even if the person who harmed you is unwilling or unable to make amends and ask for forgiveness, it is possible, and can be helpful, to forgive him. But it is certainly easier to forgive, and you, the partner, are far more likely to continue a relationship with the person, if he takes responsibility for his actions, seeks forgiveness, and makes amends.

Most therapists agree that a sign of recovery for an addict is when he is able to take full responsibility for what he has done. Judith Herman, author of *Trauma and Recovery: The Aftermath of Violence-From Domestic Abuse to Political Terror*, states "true forgiveness cannot be granted until the perpetrator has sought and earned it though confession, repentance, and restitution." In *The Unburdened Heart*, Mariah Burton-Nelson agrees that forgiveness requires confession and restitution, but adds that if reconciliation of an intimate relationship is desired, then remorse is also necessary. In his book, *The Science of Trust*, John Gottman agrees that the first phase of work for healing to occur for the victim of a betrayal and for the marriage is for the perpetrator of the betrayal to express remorse, establish ways to be transparent in all the perpetrator does in order to create understanding, acceptance and start the path towards forgiveness.

Confession is disclosing while taking full responsibility for what the person has done. It is tempting to confess by phone or via a letter sent through the mail or a text. It takes more courage to be accountable face-to-face, to directly confront the other person's expression of pain or anger or grief—but that is the more effective and desirable way to do it. The addict's therapist will advise him that preparing by first writing a letter is a good idea: A letter or written work helps the addict stay on track. He will most likely read the letter to you. It is also okay for you to write a letter *that you* read aloud to the addict and then give it to him/her. Reading the letter also provides a starting and stopping place so that interrupting and getting off track is not as easy.

Taking responsibility for one's actions and demonstrating remorse makes the addict's disclosure more effective than just dumping on you. Genuine remorse includes verifying those things that you may have suspected all along but that your mate was lying about. You are likely to feel that you don't really know this person and can't trust him. This is a natural consequence of the trauma of deception and betrayal that you have experienced. It will take time and ongoing transparency by your mate (no more secrets) for you to really accept that his (or her) behavior has changed.

Disclosure is the first step of restitution, a process that will be described further in Chapter 9. In the following example, Dan is a person who was willing to admit what he had done, but had trouble taking responsibility:

Dan had been married to Delia for ten years. Over the years he had alternated between excessive use of alcohol, cocaine, and nicotine and was an occasional gambler. Eventually he settled on a combination of heavy cigarette smoking while drinking and masturbating to pornography. Dan had been in therapy and even gone to treatment before for his alcohol use but did not come clean to the treatment team or to Delia about the extent of his compulsive sexual activities After treatment he would act contrite, go to 12-step meetings and talk to his AA sponsor, but he never did fully disclose to anyone the range of his addictive behaviors. Eventually, the desire to start acting out sexually would return along with his cocaine use. Dan and Delia separated for six months following one of his binge uses while he was gambling. His persistent efforts to woo her back and his declarations of evidence that he was attending 12-step meetings eventually persuaded Delia to give the marriage another try.

A year after their reconciliation, Dan fell into a pattern of using cocaine, then masturbating to Internet pornography or visiting chat rooms where the conversations were sexually explicit. He eventually began emailing and texting women he met in chat rooms on the computer. Caught in fantasy, he eventually became infatuated with a young woman who lived 2,000 miles away, and flew across the country to meet her. It wasn't long before Delia discovered his porn use and the long distance encounter. This time Delia filed for divorce. After a month of a long distance romance, Dan realized what he had lost. He begged Delia to let him return. He said he was sorry, he'd do anything to make it up to her, and he suggested that they go see a therapist for a session in which Delia could tell him all the ways he had hurt her, while he would listen without defending himself. Delia declined; she had already told him dozens of times over the years how his behavior was affecting her. What she wanted was to hear *him* describe how he had hurt her and express remorse, and this he said he couldn't do. They divorced.

It is surely easier for you to tell the addict how his or her secrets have affected you. You undoubtedly have a long list that you've been thinking about for a long time, and in fact may have tried to tell him more than once how you feel. If you did, you may have felt unheard. So it is much more beneficial for you to listen to the addict, telling *you* how he believes he's hurt you and impacted your life. His ability to validate your reality through his understanding of what he did to you, and then his willingness to say he was wrong and is truly sorry are huge steps in demonstrating remorse.

This is so important that it is useful to have a therapist guide him, but not everyone has access to therapists with experience in disclosure with addicts and partners. A helpful alternative is to have a sponsor or other support person facilitate the disclosure. It is critical for you to have support afterward, and it is likely you may not want that support to come from the addict. This is normal, and after you have had a chance to process what you have heard, you will likely get to the point where you will want your mate's support, but not initially.

A word of caution: If you've been the subject of an unexpected disclosure and are experiencing a great deal of anger, it may be tempting to run and tell your children about their father's behavior and how it hurt you. Do not do this! You are likely to regret it, but will be unable to undo the damage. Disclosure to children should be carefully planned. If possible, it is best done by the addict either alone or with you, and in age-appropriate ways that are meaningful for their developmental stage. This will be discussed in the next chapter.

Finally, honor your spouse's courage in being willing to come clean, and your own courage in being willing to listen. The willingness by both of you to participate in this process is itself a hopeful sign for the future of your relationship.

What to Expect if Your Mate Goes Into Addiction Treatment

If your mate has been "discovered" or has partially disclosed to you and has gone to treatment, most treatment centers have family therapy that you will be asked to attend. You will probably listen to lectures or see DVDs that teach you about addiction and/or partners' reactions and behaviors. This can be very useful because you get a chance to see that your behavior often plays a role in the addiction. It's not that you have *caused* the addict's behavior—he's responsible for his own actions. It just means that you are in a "dance" with him. His behavior triggers thoughts in you that result in actions. For example, you sense that he is lying about where he has been and you start to nag him about it. Then he gets angry and frightened and reacts by telling you that you are crazy or mistaken. He acts in some way that he has learned over time will make you think that perhaps you are wrong or will lose him, so you change your behavior. Or the "dance" gets so full of anger and fear that one or both of you leaves in order to create distance. In that leaving, the addict and sometimes the partner acts out. The addict acts out by getting into his compulsive behavior. You may act out by over-functioning with the children or on your job or in the household, or perhaps by eating too much, or over-exercising and restricting food, maybe spending money, or even using drugs or having your own affair. Either in an individual session with a therapist or in a group of other family members, you will have an opportunity to talk about how you are doing.

Recently addiction professionals have become more aware that living with an addicted person – someone who lies, who attempts to discount your feelings and observations about what's going on, who at times may be verbally abusive – is traumatic for the partner. Partners of addicts are increasingly being recognized as trauma victims, and our research confirms that many of them identify themselves as this. Family week can provide an opportunity for the partner to gain validation for her feelings and to begin the process of helping her recover. This is only the beginning; most partners can benefit from continuing with therapy and support after returning home.

Most often, if the treatment center knows the full story of your spouse's addiction, they will have encouraged him or her (in some cases, demanded) to reveal to you what his behaviors were during his acting out. Ideally you will be asked how much information you want. But in the end, it is the addict's decision how much to tell you.

Steps to Preparing to Hear a Disclosure

Once some disclosure has happened at discovery, the partner generally doubts everything, is sure that the addict is not being honest, and doesn't want to ever believe the mate again for fear of being hurt. That is normal; it will take a while again for you to believe him (usually one to three years). When the addiction is to sex, most partners think they want to hear all the details—who was involved, for how long, where, what they did, how many times, was it at home, whether the sex was protected or unprotected, what the other person looked like,

THE FORMAL DISCLOSURE

what they said, and on and on. No matter what your mate says, you will probably embellish his horrible secrets with even worse betrayals. We recommend that the addict give general information and specifics about how your health may be compromised, but then let you be the guide about what details you want to know. You still have to determine how the information will help you.

Although you may want to learn everything, you must ask yourself, "What is my goal? What do I want to do with this information? Do I use it to see how my health and relationship are affected? Or to see what information I can get to measure my self-worth? Perhaps my goal is to get enough information to see if I can determine when he is acting out again so I can protect myself."

Our experience is that minute details generally serve only to make you feel worse about yourself, and will cause you to spend hours and hours obsessing about the information rather than how you got into this "dance" in the first place. It is useful to have a set of questions that you want your mate to answer. This helps you get your needs met and gives him a place from which to start. We recommend that you take the following steps in preparation for the disclosure:

1. Make a commitment to yourself to use the disclosure as a way to start the healing process for yourself. You can decide if you want to work on the relationship after you have heard what the addict has to say. Part of working on yourself is acknowledging where you have not been honest with the addict about how you feel, what you really fear.

2. Acknowledge that knowing only part of the truth hurts and that being in limbo contributes to the confusion, fear, and anger.

3. Write a letter expressing your feelings – the anger, the hurt, etc – about what you do know. Identify all the ways the addict's behavior has had an impact on you.

4. Write a boundaries letter about how you want things to be different. Review the letter with your therapist or sponsor, and then read it to your partner.

5. Formulate a set of questions that you want the addict to answer. Here are some examples:

- Are you seriously involved in a recovery program or in therapy?

- Are you committed to working on our relationship and repairing the damage? What does working on the relationship mean you are willing to do?

- When in our relationship did these activities begin and how long have they been going on?

- Have you engaged in drug use or sexual activities that may have put me at a health risk? What risky activities did you engage in, and when?

- Have you cut off all contact with using friends or sexual partners? If not, what are the obstacles to this happening, and what are your plans for overcoming these obstacles? (Ask that your mate write a note to the affair partner that makes it clear that the affair is over and that he is committed to working on the relationship. Ask to see it before he sends it. Or ask that he make a phone call with you or the therapist in the room when he calls.)

- Have you been using or sexually involved with any people that I know? If so, with whom?

- What significant lies have you told me to cover up your activities?

- Can you think of arguments we had in which you blamed me when the real issue was your acting out?

The Timing and Extent of Formal Disclosure

In our survey, we asked addicts and partners for their recommendations regarding optimal timing of a formal disclosure. The results varied, often based on their personal experience. Two years after her partner first disclosed to her, one woman advised:

> *Do it soon, and in the safety of a supportive environment, such as a therapist's office. Be fearlessly honest, but not detailed. Be willing to share without regard to consequences that might affect honesty. Try to understand your partner's feelings without judging them or closing down. Realize you are valuable and lovable, regardless of what anyone says or does. Look at being honest as a gift you*

give yourself. You can say, "That's who I really am." Give others the choice to decide to like you or not, to be with you or not.

We agree this is good advice.

Disclosure of Relapse

Not all partners want to know everything, especially partners who have been through many admissions and are so angry or fragile they don't believe that can hear anymore. This is true of partners of addicts who have relapsed numerous times. However, learning of your partner's relapse from him rather than by later discovering it is ultimately helpful for the relationship. Our research clearly shows that in cases in which the addict discloses before the partner discovers a relapse, these couples report more satisfying relationships and more willingness by the partner to support the addict getting back into recovery.

The next hardest disclosure is to children. Addicts sometimes find it is even harder than coming clean to the partner. Although it is difficult, disclosure to children is very important. How to do it depends on each child's circumstances and needs. The next chapter discusses how to explain things to children.

References

Burton-Nelson, Mariah. *The Unburdened Heart*. San Francisco: Harper, 2000.

Gottman, John. *The Science of Trust: Emotional Attunement for Couples*. New York: Norton, 2011.

Herman, Judith. *Trauma and Recovery: The Aftermath of Violence—From Domestic Abuse to Political Terror*. New York: Basic Books, 1992

Chapter Six
What to Tell the Kids

Disclosing family secrets of all types to children is one of the most difficult tasks parents encounter. It may be harder for an addict to reveal his or her sexual acting out, drug use, or other addictive behavior to the child than to his partner. Addicts feel shame, anger, fear of alienating the children, fear that the children might be harmed by the information, and concern that they might tell others. Some partners, too, resist telling the children for fear they will blame the partner or feel shame at the possibility they might tell others.

In describing families of sex addicts, Earle and Earle wrote in 1995,

> "The secrets of parents cannot help but prove destructive to the child. No matter how deeply hidden or repressed by their parents, these secrets affect children. Secrets creep into every aspect of family living, creating high levels of psychological stress, pressure, and tension. The energy focused on keeping secrets does not allow children to be fully present. Children may not even be consciously aware of the family secrets, but these secrets seldom escape the unconscious." (pg. 118)

People who are unwilling to share with their children often assume that the children did not know what was going on. In fact, children often know; research has shown that about two-thirds of children know something about a parent's sexual acting out before disclosure. They may have overheard telephone calls, arguments, and conversations. They may have seen pornography on a parent's computer or iPhone, but may have kept the information to themselves. Even if they didn't know the details, they may have sensed the stress and tension between their parents.

Yet experts have tried to educate us for many years about the importance of appropriate sharing with children. Psychiatrist Carl Jung wrote in 1969, "Telling children about your struggles helps them developmentally to have a realistic picture of what it means to be human." By telling older children about the addiction and recovery you can validate the children's feelings. Furthermore, it gives them permission to talk about what they may have felt and experienced during their parents' acting out.

It is important to note, however, that what we and others advocate is appropriate disclosure. Some partners blurt out information prematurely and in ways that blame the addict. They do this in order to get validation and support from their children, or as a means of expressing their anger at the addict and punishing him (or her). Such admissions often result in distancing the children from the addict, and partners who have done this usually subsequently regret it. In this chapter we will describe what an appropriate disclosure is.

Effect of Parental Addiction on the Children

A parent's addiction can have a major impact on the children. People who suffer from all varieties of addiction are consumed with planning, obtaining, using, or recovering from the effects of their drug of choice. They then cover up their behavior and their shame and pain with lies and secrets. This behavior ignites the emotional distress of the partner. You may understandably become obsessed with discovering evidence and catching the addict, reel with anger and put up emotional walls to stay detached, or pursue the addict with clingy behaviors. This behavior contributes to the emotional distress of the addict. Both parents mismanage the emotions that keep them trapped in addictive and sometimes codependent behaviors and intense shame. Often these parents are unavailable for the children emotionally and, at times, physically.

To compensate for their own insecurities and to reduce anxiety, addicted parents may engage in several different types of unhealthy behaviors with their children. They can be over-controlling, establishing rigid rules for children that are confusing and unrealistic. Addicted parents may use destructive criticism of the child to cover their own pain and shame. This shame sets up a family system with rigidly defined boundaries in which secrets are expected to be kept, rejection is common, people are self-focused, maturity is rarely modeled and underdeveloped, and everyone—parents and children—lacks a sense of security.

Some children may attempt to solve parental problems by overachieving and being the "perfect" child, or by not rocking the boat in hopes of keeping the peace. Other kids take the opposite route—they are rebellious or engage in problematic behaviors to draw attention away from the parents' problems. An 18-year-old boy, in treatment for marijuana and alcohol addiction, related,

> *No matter what I did, it wasn't enough. I used to make the best grades, was captain of the swim team, even won a medal at a debate a couple of years ago. They didn't even notice, but if I make one B the shit hits the fan. So I figured what's the use? I'd just get high and see what they thought about that! That's when my drug use first started.*

It is common for addicted people to have more than one significant relationship or marriage while they're using. Most single addicts, especially relationship addicts, become involved in serial relationships. Anxious for their children to accept their new partner, they bring this new person into the home soon after meeting him or her. If one or both members of the new couple are acting out sexually, the home environment is quickly sexualized. The couple may talk openly about the sexual desire for each other, touch each other in sexually explicit ways, or have little regard for the sexual sounds that can be overheard by children even through closed bedroom doors. If you and the addict are no longer living together and (s)he is dating, you may have to deal with your children's distress at what they are observing when with their addicted parent.

Sometimes the new partner is very attentive to the child. This can be very confusing for the child because of loyalty to the addict's former mate. The child may try to please the parent and becomes attached to the new partner, and then experiences another loss when the addict parent moves on to yet another new partner.

Partners and addicts may make a child a confidant or even a surrogate spouse. These young people are given information and attention that are confusing and frequently far more sexualized or sophisticated than they can understand. Children hear and see the accusations and denials, the frightening fights, and the loud silence of stonewalling. Sometimes they see parents hit one another when anger gets mismanaged. Sometimes kids get hit as well.

Children may witness or find evidence of the drug use, gambling, or sexual acting out and are coerced to keep secrets about the addict's behavior with threats that to tell will result in the family breaking up or with Dad going to jail. Sometimes a child finds an Internet pornography file or emails from a sexual chat room on the home computer, or parent's iPad or Smartphone, and is faced with confronting the parent, telling the other parent, or holding onto the secret over time. When teens reach puberty, this secret-keeping can turn into intense rage and some teens even threaten to blackmail the addict parent. As the partner who may not realize what is happening, you may find yourself trying to cope with an angry acting-out child who is unwilling to open up to about his feelings.

As discussed in previous chapters, some addicts act out in illegal ways and the disclosures happen through other sources such as police, attorneys, the spouse of an affair partner, or the media. The list is long and the potential for children to hear about the addictive behavior from other sources is greater than you might expect. Therefore, disclosure from you and the addict is helpful to your relationship with the child. Your addicted spouse should be the primary source of information, but it is very helpful if you are involved as well. Disclosure is the first step in helping your children deal with the adverse consequences of other people's judgments and behaviors and their disappointment in you or your mate.

Contrary to what the media would have you believe, most children within a sexually addicted family are not overtly sexually abused. However, some are exposed to the sex addict's behaviors and use the behaviors as the seeds of their own sexual unfolding. Some adolescents and young adults find themselves caught up in sexual acting out and drug use that is similar to the ways the parent acted out.

Drug addicts sometimes use drugs in front of their children. Despite strict laws prohibiting adults from providing minors with illegal substances, some parents in addicted families even offer their kids drugs. It is common for addicts to reveal that their own parents smoked marijuana with them, or gave them alcohol at a very young age, or shared prescription medications. This modeling can send a mixed message about the inappropriateness and hazards of drug use or out-of-control behaviors by minors.

It is common for children in homes with eating disorders or out-of-control spending or gambling to watch an adult engage in destructive behavior. They often see the consequences and feel helpless to change things despite valiant efforts to do so.

> *My Dad always seemed lucky at cards and brought home lots of cash from the horse races. What I didn't know though was that he lost lots more, he just didn't bother to tell us. He used my college money to gamble with and lost. My grandmother gave me that money and it wasn't his. Mom told me that he had been betting on the horses on the Internet and now we have to pay back what he lost. Things are bad between them. If they just wouldn't fight maybe this would work out somehow. I hate it when they fight.*
>
> —17-year-old daughter of gambling addict

Any type of addictive behavior in a household is destructive to children, but making children the object of sexual acting out is one of the most problematic. Fear of abandonment or pain combined with the special attention of the parent makes this the perfect double bind for the child. While they fear the pain, they crave the attention and long to be special to the parent. It is common for adult survivors to describe how they feared and dreaded the sexual encounter with a parent, but at the same time how seductive was the pleasure of the attention and being told "you're special."

> *I'd stare at the door and hope it wouldn't open. When it did and he came over, I knew what to do, what he wanted. I hated the way he smelled, and can remember these sounds he'd make; when the sounds would start, I'd just go somewhere else [in my head] until I'd hear him say, "You're my girl, my best girl. I love you the most because you're special." As much as I hate him for what he did to me, I am ashamed to say I longed to see that look on his face the next day when he'd smile that smile—it was the only time I've ever felt like somebody. Later he told me he was addicted to me. I don't know what that means.*
>
> —20-year-old after leaving home, remembers abuse happening between ages 11 and 13

Because children are dependent on us, they feel they have few choices but to participate, often blaming themselves for what has happened. If they witness the abuse of another child, the guilt and pain are even more debilitating and long lasting. If your child is being sexually abused by your addict spouse, it is very possible that your child will be very angry at you for not protecting him or her, even if you are truly unaware of what was going on. This is something that will take a long time in therapy for the two of you to work out.

When children's boundaries have been violated, especially by sexual abuse, they don't develop boundaries for anything. They often take on "protecting" someone else because they feel powerless to protect themselves. They don't recognize that their bodies are their own or that they have any say about what happens to them. They then become easy prey for someone else who has boundary issues themselves. It's not surprising that we see young people pairing up with unsuitable partners with whom they essentially repeat what happened to them in their family of origin.

Children raised in addicted families often have a variety of adverse experiences in childhood. We have touched on some of those categories in descriptions above. Specifically the Centers for Disease Control (CDC) categorize adverse experiences in childhood as being victim of emotional, physical, or sexual abuse, living in an addicted household, living with someone who is chronically depressed or suicidal, or living in a household where the mother was treated with violence, a parent was incarcerated, separated or divorced. The CDC has well documented that there are enduring health and behavioral effects of childhood maltreatment (Anda, et al., 2005). These effects include an increase in substance abuse, early and impersonal sexual intercourse, greater than 50 sexual partners in a lifetime, increased use of nicotine, staying in relationships after they have become violent, post-traumatic stress reactions, and a host of physical problems including irritable bowel syndrome, unexplained panic, anxiety, and depression, and even increase in hypertension, and asthma. While this might scare you, it is important to realize that your children are affected in all sorts of ways because they live in an addicted household.

Addicted families are what Merle Fossum and Marilyn Mason, in *Facing Shame: Families in Recovery*, called shame-bound families.

Their description provides an excellent overview of the dynamics of such families:

> . . . *A shame-bound family is a family with a self-sustaining, multigenerational system of interaction among a cast of characters who are (or were in their lifetime) loyal to a set of rules and injunctions demanding control, perfectionism, blame and denial. The pattern inhibits or defeats the development of authentic intimate relationships, promotes secrets and vague personal boundaries, unconsciously instills shame in the family members, as well as chaos in their lives and binds them to perpetuate the shame in themselves and their kin. It does so regardless of the good intentions, wishes, and love which may also be a part of the system.*

In all cases of any kind of abuse, especially sexual abuse, the addict must be accountable for his actions, so some form of disclosure and acknowledgment is important for the child and the addict to heal. This is true even if the child is an adult by the time the addict gets enough recovery to take responsibility. You and your child will also most likely have to work through his or her feelings about you. The capacity of a parent to have a coherent and cohesive narrative about life's experiences and ability to reflect on and take responsibility for his or her behavior can actually interrupt the intergenerational transmission of psychopathology while building resilience in a child (Fonagy, et al., 1995, Siegel 1999).

To get in touch with the impact of your addiction on your child, think about or list ways your child has been exposed to addiction.

What do you think the impact this may have had on your child or evidence you already see of how this has impacted your child? In what ways was your child used?

How, What, and How Much Do We Tell

An impulsive disclosure to a child is yet another way children are impacted in negative ways as a result of addiction. Sometimes an addicted parent is forced to acknowledge behaviors because a child discovers the evidence, or another person tells or is going to tell part of the story (such as an angry or concerned partner, neighbor, relative, or information in the media) and it is important for the child to hear the truth from the addict in an age-appropriate way. Ideally a well-planned event with both parents involved, that has been reviewed and practiced in a therapeutic setting or with a sponsor, is the way to go. Unfortunately, that is not always possible.

Disclosure is best done after consideration of the following:

- When should we do this – soon after the addict tells the partner? Or do we wait until the addict has some recovery and/or the partner has calmed down?
- What do we do if it's on TV or in the newspaper?
- Who should be present – the addict alone, the partner alone, both? With the therapist?
- Should the kids be told together, or individually?
- What do children of various ages want or need to be told?
- How much do we tell the child?
- What information is private, just between the addict and partner, and what makes sense to talk to our kids about?
- How do we help our children be prepared for what others might say or ask?

In order to be able to give good advice to parents about whether or not to disclose, how much information to give, and what to expect after talking with the child, we conducted several surveys of sex addicts and partners who indeed had had to make decisions about if, when, and how to reveal to their children. Respondents reported a variety of circumstances, ranging from forced disclosure (because of arrest, threats by others to reveal, or insistence by the partner), to a well-planned event in a therapeutic environment. Below are a few examples from parents who participated in our past research published in an article (Corley & Schneider, 2003). The first is of a disclosure done very early, and by the partner alone, without the addict's participation or presence. She disclosed to both of her children, but spoke to each one at a time in an age-appropriate manner.

> *Within one month after discovery of my husband's behaviors, I told my older son, who was 11 at the time, that his father was addicted*

> to pornography and that it was harmful to our relationship because pornography objectifies women. I told him about it at home without anyone else present. I told my daughter, who was 7 that we were having problems, that Daddy and Mommy needed help, and that we were getting it. My son was tearful and scared, afraid we would separate. He was able to ask me questions about sex, pornography, and addiction. My daughter tried to cheer everyone else up, a budding codependent, but later was able to discuss her feelings of fear. I told the children different things because I thought the little one was too young to understand, but I talked to her about it when she turned 10. My son apparently blocked out the disclosure of his father's sexual addiction, and three years later claimed he didn't know about it.

A convicted sex offender wrote,

> I think it depends on the addict's own recovery progress and the age of the children. If the addict is staying sober and is motivated to recover, and the kids are at a minimum teenagers, it's the right time. If the public is notified of a sex offender, the addict should disclose before the public is informed. The child should hear about the offending behaviors from the parent and not through other sources.

When disclosure is a choice, the positive reasons for doing so include validating what the child already knows, divulging before others tell, hope of breaking the cycle of addiction, and for the child's safety (Black et al, 2003). Unfortunately, some explanations to children are impulsively done by partners who want to punish the errant addict or who want the children to side with them rather than the addict. Others are forced by circumstances, such as public disclosure, and the parents have very little time to reflect on their fears or concerns. Here is an account of the experience of a 17-year old son of an addict whose father was a federal judge:

> My Dad beat up this drug dealer who was with a prostitute and he was arrested. That's how my Mom found out that he was a sex addict and a drug addict. Then he talked to me and my sister. That went okay. I was really mad at first, but my Dad seemed so changed after he went to treatment that it was good. It really prepared us for

what was about to happen. He's a big shot in our town—or at least he was until this happened. When he went to court, the newspapers and TV stations got word of his deal and they printed this trash about him in the paper—it was even on the TV news. My folks knew it was going to happen and we all got together and decided what we were going to say to people. The news media got the old "no comment" line like you see on TV, but with friends it was hard. Everybody was tweeting about it, saying really horrible things about my Dad and some about me. At first I was really embarrassed but then some of my friends were really cool and supported me against some other freaks at school. It isn't such a big deal now. I am proud about how we all got through it."

Children's reactions to Disclosure (Parents' description)

Before describing how best to disclose to children, we would like to relate the parents' perception of how children react. Most children's initial reactions to revelations of a parent's sexual acting, drug use, or gambling are perceived as negative. Usually children are shocked, and in disbelief; some say the information validates their suspicions or actual knowledge. This turns to fear and sadness because they are worried that their parents will separate or divorce and are concerned about what will happen to them. Many older children express anger towards the addict and try to support the partner; often they voice anger about the impact on their lives. Sometimes this results in their own acting out in dangerous or addictive ways or anxious attempts to cheer everyone up or comfort one or both parents. Occasionally a child will praise the addict for getting help or the couple for appearing to work together to solve problems. Although at the time of disclosure some children appeared to understand, months or years later were surprised when told again. This is more likely to be true of younger children

Below are some examples of what parents reported to us. This mother of older children described the aftermath of a disclosure that was forced by a young adult's suspicions. It resulted in the entire family getting into treatment. Premature disclosure by the addict led to additional traumatic events, but eventually the family adjusted.

WHAT TO TELL THE KIDS

My young adult daughter became increasingly suspicious and began asking questions. When she and I were alone in the car one day, she asked me outright if Dad had had affairs, and I answered yes. This was the catalyst to us getting into recovery. Two months later, my 22-year old son noticed some Twelve-Step books lying around and asked questions. We set up an appointment with our therapist to have a controlled disclosure, but then my husband inappropriately pulled him aside and dumped it on him when they were alone in a car. My 13-year old son was told soon thereafter in a planned disclosure by his father in the therapist's office with the entire family present.

My daughter's reaction was anger and tears. She wanted more information. She needed lots of time and emotion for weeks and weeks. She wouldn't talk to [her] dad – she wanted to be with me all the time. My 22-year old son told his father he didn't want any more information, but he wanted me to tell him more. Two days later my husband missed an important family appointment, and in response my son slit his wrist. It was a major event – ambulance, emergency room... When my 13-year old son was told, he cried, and said, "It feels like my family is falling apart." He asked no questions.

Now we are open at home and my son hears talk about addiction and about our counseling and Twelve-Step groups. I often ask him if he has questions, and he always says no. My older children ask me specific questions about the addiction and broad questions about how their dad is doing. My husband is still not open and comfortable talking with the kids, but they do both speak with him about Twelve-Step groups.

A 55-year -year old physician, whose acting out had included internet pornography and prostitution, disclosed to his 3 children, ages 10-19 years old, a short time after telling his wife, who then asked him to leave. The disclosure took place in the home, with all family members present.

I told them I had violated my wife's trust and that we would be separating. I told them I would be in therapy to resolve the problem. Only the youngest said anything. On the verge of tears, he asked how long I would be gone. They were otherwise shocked and speechless.

Timing of Disclosure to Children

It is surprising how many parents do not disclose to their children, despite awareness of the value of doing so. Most parents choose not to tell, delay telling, or disclose with trepidation. The addicts in our study had four primary concerns that fueled their decision not to tell. The main concern was fear of loss of the relationship with the partner or child. Early on in recovery, the partner is fragile and these addicts wanted her to gain more recovery before divulging difficult material. This was especially true when the addicted person needed to acknowledge that he had acted out with men as part of his addiction or had determined he was gay. Partners said they postponed disclosure until they were not so angry and wanted evidence that the addict was serious about his or her recovery.

Some addicts feared the partner might use the information in a custody battle. This is a legitimate concern – we have seen several cases in which the information used in a disclosure was then used against the addict in custody hearings. However, if a disclosure is well planned, often the results are that the child actually sees that the addict is taking responsibility for his or her action.

Some addicts and partners reported that they felt the child was too young to understand or that the child was so out of control with his or her own behavior, the parents did not want to add fuel to the fire.

All these reasons are important. If you are fortunate enough to have escaped forced or impulsive disclosure, so that you have an opportunity to work through the above factors, both of you can benefit from discussing them with a therapist and planning the timing and content of the event so as to minimize the adverse consequences. Our research and clinical experience concludes that it depends on the circumstances of your situation. Both partners and addicts agree that is it important that both of them are working on their own issues as well as working together on some level as co-parents. At the same time, it's important not to wait too long because the children already can see and feel that something is wrong. It's a good thing to say as a couple you are having some problems but are trying to work on those problems, and that none of what is going on is the fault of the children.

What should you do if you believe it is definitely time for the children to get some information, but the addict is unwilling to disclose? Let's say you have attempted to discuss the importance of disclosure with the addict, but without getting anywhere. Even if your marriage is over and the only option is for <u>you</u> to disclose to them, the addict is still your children's father, so that your disclosure needs to be carefully thought out. You don't want to further damage their relationship with the addict. It's a good idea for you to discuss this situation with a therapist. If the addict is cooperative, disclosing together will give him (or her) some support, and will convey to the children that the two of you are still cooperating in doing what's best for them.

What Kids Want to Know

After hearing an apology letter read to him in a disclosure session with his parents and the therapist, a 15-year-old boy related,

> *My Dad and Mom asked me to talk to them. My Dad said he had done some things wrong and needed to talk to me about that. He read me a letter and said he was a sex addict. We had talked about addiction at school and sex addiction was mentioned but I really didn't know what that was. He told me he'd lied to Mom and to us kids and that he was wrong to do that. He had gotten involved with other women and spent lots of time looking at pornography like people drink or use drugs, instead of figuring out how to solve his problems. He says that is why he goes to meetings, so he can learn to solve his problems. He apologized for leaving his porn where I could see it and said that it was a bad thing to look at pictures of women and make them into objects. Things like that. He said he was sorry that he had been gone all the time and that he hadn't made it to my baseball games or track meets.*
>
> *I guess what I remember most is that he said he was sorry, that it was wrong to lie and that he loved me and he would try to do better. I believe him.*

That was an example of a disclosure well done.

Based on our studies and clinical experience we know it is not necessary to disclose to very young children. They may understand the concept of lying or breaking a promise, but the concept of addiction is beyond their cognitive ability. Below is a list of suggestions about what kids want to know, by age:

<u>Pre-school, ages 3-5</u>

These children have often been witness to fighting or have heard that you are an addict and don't know what is happening. They want to know:

- Are you going to die or leave me?
- Am I in trouble?
- Do you love me?
- Do I have to do something to fix this?

They need guidelines and structure about their behavior. This is when consistency counts from you. Because your mate has been out-of-control (and perhaps that is true of you too) doesn't mean they get to be out-of-control. When their confusion results in tantrums or rule breaking for attention, connect with them and then redirect their behavior. (Too often sex-addicted families get hypervigilant and worry about a child's normal sexual exploration and genital stimulation. See Debra Haffner's *From Diapers to Dating* for excellent information about what is normal.)

<u>Early Elementary (ages 5-6)</u>

- Is this my fault?
- Will something bad happen? (divorce fear)
- Who are you and your spouse now? Your mate (the addict) is now very different and this child has learned to adapt to deprivation.

They need encouragement to talk about how they feel and reassurance that none of what is happening is their fault. Drawing pictures and then talking is good way to get the conversation going. Some children fall back on best behaviors in hopes that if you divorce they are not abandoned. Letting them know exactly when you will be with them and good follow through is important.

WHAT TO TELL THE KIDS

<u>Upper elementary/middle school (9–13)</u>

- Am I normal?
- Will I get this addiction because I have sexual feelings?
- Am I going to end up a drug addict because my Dad [the addict] is?
- What will happen to me if you get divorced?.

Pre-teens are concerned about being normal anyway, so dealing with the addiction adds to those worries. Helping them with facts about changes in their bodies and brains of this stage in life can give reassurance. It is also helpful to explain that addiction is an unhealthy way to cope with emotional distress and that you need to learn together other ways to cope when either of you is upset. If separation or a divorce is likely, be honest that it is a possibility but that no firm decision has been made until you and your partner have had time to figure things out; emphasize that no matter what happens you will still be their dad or mom and will always love them.

<u>Teen/Adult years</u>

- How could Dad do this to you? To the family?
- How does this specifically relate to me? (Dad has ruined my life!)

Listen to the feelings of your teen or grown children. Ask questions about their fear or anger. Seek to understand and stay connected. It is important to reinforce or clarify family rules. Even if you have been a rule breaker in the past, your job is still to be the parent in the present.

In contrast to the above list, here are the things that kids <u>don't</u> want to know:

- The specific details of your mate's acting out
- How angry you are at your spouse
- How sex is between you and your spouse or anyone else

Generally, small children do not need disclosure or explanation about addiction. An apology for not being around or being preoccupied is appropriate, but mostly they need good parenting. Older children can benefit from information about sex addiction and addiction in general. There is some genetic predisposition for addiction. Because your mate an addict, your children are likely to have an increased risk; therefore, discussing your mate's addiction with older children (optimally with both of you present) is appropriate and disclosure is one way to do this

Because children of different ages need different types of information, you need to consider this when planning your disclosure. If your children's ages aren't close together, it is probably best to disclose separately to each one. And of course, in such cases you need to take into account how to give an older child information that you don't want him or her to tell the younger child. None of this is easy.

What and how much to tell becomes the challenge. And how can you be both accountable and a good parent? There are no perfect answers for how you tell kids or what you divulge. We are going to recommend a process instead of telling you all the "right" things to say. We will give you some concrete examples, but this disclosure has to fit your situation.

First and foremost, your job as a good parent is to make your love visible by providing structure, guidance, protection, and nurturing in healthy ways. It is to help your child integrate the feelings about what has happened to her during your spouse's addiction with her thoughts and help her plan future actions about her feelings. This is a difficult task since many partners had little or no modeling from their parents on these topics. If this is true for you, you may need to do some homework. Figuring this out starts with a foundation—a foundation made up of your values and then learning some new skills

It also means getting rid of faulty core beliefs. That takes time and requires taking active steps to change how you think, which changes how you feel, and in turn increases your chances of changing what you do. Most addicts have a set of negative beliefs about self that need to be corrected to a set of hopeful, positive beliefs that people in recovery utilize. A sample of negative core beliefs outlined in *Out of the Shadows* by Patrick Carnes are representative of what many addicts report as fueling their distorted thinking and destructive values.

- I am basically a bad, unworthy person.

- No one would love me as I am.

- My needs are never going to be met if I have to depend on others.
- Sex (alcohol, drugs, food, gambling) is my most important need.

Many partners have also grown up with some negative core beliefs, which may have been strengthened by the trauma that many partners experienced:

- I am not a worthwhile person
- No one would love me for myself
- I can control other people's behavior
- Sex is the most important sign of love

Think about how your core beliefs have influenced your value system. Perhaps you are not sure what your values are or you may want to change or improve your values. Here are a few questions to get you started.

- Where did you get your values? Parents? Other family members? Teachers? Preachers/Rabbis/Leaders in the faith community you were raised in?
- Which values that you learned in childhood can serve you well now?
- Are there values you learned that are not respectful of your personal growth or recovery? What faulty beliefs were generated from those messages?
- How would you change or adapt both the beliefs and values to better suit you as a strong person in recovery who is also a responsible parent?
- Review your values with your mate/co-parent. Together list the values you both want to guide you in creating structure, guidance, protection, and nurturing for your children (and yourselves!).

It will be helpful for you to list statements that counter or refute those core beliefs above. Let this new set of values help you develop those counter statements.

Your values as a person in recovery and new core beliefs that reflect those values can make everything easier if you actually follow them.

In the past you may have been covering up for your addicted spouse. What were the values that guided your behavior then? What values do you want to guide you now? There is something very empowering about being honest.

Here's an example of what the addict might say to a younger child:

> *Your Mom and I have been fighting because I have been telling lies to her. Because I have lied, Mom doesn't trust me and she has every right to be mad. What I did was wrong—lying to her was wrong. Sometimes I even lied to you about working when I was off doing stuff with people I should not have been with. When I should have been with your Mom and you, I chose to find some other people to be with when I felt mad, or sad, or lonely. Sometimes I would drink and do things that were dangerous and then lie to Mom about what I was doing when she was worried about me. Now I go to meetings at night to learn better ways to make decisions when I am feeling sad, or mad. What I did was very hurtful to your Mom and to our family—including you. It will take your Mom a long time to start trusting me again and she has every right to be mad at me. You did not do anything wrong. Neither did Mommy. I was the one who did things that were wrong. I am sorry I hurt her and that I have not been around much to spend time with you. I love you.*

Let's look at how this fits our previous discussions of parenting in terms of structure, guidance, protection, and nurturing. Think about marriage or a committed relationship. You might list your values about being in a marriage. You might want to write the messages you want to send to your children to guide them about marriage and commitment in what you say and do.

It is common to feel guilty about the difficulties in your home, your distractibility at times, and what may now feel like inadequate parenting; you may overcompensate by letting children run all over you. This is especially true when they reach their teen years and will use your mate's addiction history to manipulate both of you. But your job as a parent is to provide *structure* to *protect* your child. Sometimes you have to be firm and say,

> *I can see that you don't think it's fair that you are not allowed to "hook up" (or date) now, and that you think that because Dad was*

irresponsible in his addiction, you should be able to do dangerous things now. The rule in our house is that children do not drive cars or go to parties or get-togethers without an adult who is chaperoning until they are 16 because we value your life. Since it is our job to protect you the best we can, and the odds are greater that you will get hurt if you drive or party with friends at this early age without a parent supervising, you will have to wait until you are older and have more experience with life. Since you are 14 and have acted pretty mature at times, we agree that we will talk about when you can go with a group to an event without us, but for now—no "hooking up" or dating alone. I see that you are angry and that's normal when someone is hoping to do something special and it has to be postponed. It's okay to be angry and we have talked about ways to deal with anger in the past. I have confidence in you and think you will get beyond the anger and decide how you want to be with your friends in ways that fit our values and rules.

Certainly some 14 year olds will ignore this and do it anyway. But, if they know your values, the rules, and the reasons behind them, it is more likely than not they will follow your rule. It is also valuable to give your kids a way out; sometimes kids don't want to do something that a peer is pressuring them to do. By co-creating a code sentence or phrase so when they call and use that phrase you know it means that they need to be picked up or that they want you to say no to a request.

Nurturance means that you take time out to spend with your children. No matter how old kids are, they need to know they have some special time with you as an adult, as somebody who loves and cares about them and listens. If you go to the movies with your children but rarely have any one-on-one time to talk and listen to each other, time with your children is not as valuable as it could be. Going to the movies together is better than nothing at all, but taking time to talk about what is going on in their lives and how they feel is important for people to feel valued.

Feeling valued translates into healthy families. Mark Laaser contrasts unhealthy and healthy families in his book *Healing the Wounds of Sexual Addiction*. As you review the characteristics of healthy and unhealthy families in the next paragraph, think about the values you were raised with and have operated with and see what if anything you want to change.

In unhealthy families boundaries are either very rigid or nonexistent. In healthy families boundaries are firm but flexible. Parents care and nurture each other and their children. There is personal respect for boundaries. In unhealthy families, the rules are centered on keeping the secret, so people are not to acknowledge what is going on. It is the "don't ask, don't tell" rule so you just don't talk. With that rule comes the injunction not to feel anything, to blame others for your problems, to minimize and deny that problems even exist unless it will get you something. Children in these families take on roles that are rigid and defined.

In healthy families, children's roles are more flexible, but the parents stay in the adult position so children have a chance to grow and mature over time. People take personal responsibility for their actions, and honesty is rewarded. People talk and feel, and accept that problems are inevitable in life and can be dealt with, and these folks can ask for help. People listen to each other, individuality and teamwork are both supported and encouraged, and feelings are accepted. Physical self-care is modeled and taught, children feel safe and know that they can always come home. Basic needs are provided for. Healthy families learn to cope with and express a full range of emotions. Spirituality plays an important role in daily living.

How to Help Your Child Do Well

As shown in some research in the area of prevention education, some basic characteristics are consistently seen in children who do well in the world. These can help you shape your parenting plan. Children who are successful as adults (and during childhood) have high emotional intelligence. Daniel Goleman, author of *Emotional Intelligence*, describes people with high emotional IQ as having five specific abilities:

1. The ability to recognize a feeling when it happens

2. The ability to handle feelings in appropriate or self-enhancing ways

3. The ability to motivate self to delay gratification and stifle impulses

4. The ability to recognize emotional states of others (having empathy)

5. The ability to respond rather than react to emotional states of others

Researchers are finding that these skills can be taught to children (and adults), who then improve in many areas of their lives. In fact, children who have good impulse control (#3) are less likely to become addicts. It makes sense when you think about how addicts are so impulsive with their actions.

Daniel Siegel, a researcher and psychiatrist, has written many books about the brain and how to help children learn to use both sides of their brains so as to have better emotional intelligence. In his book, *The Whole Brain Child* (2011) he talks about the importance of helping your child use all parts of his brain to deal with emotional situations. He points out that the brain has specific parts that have specific jobs. The left side of the brain helps you organize thoughts and think logically, while the right side helps you experience emotions and read other people's non-verbal communications. He also reminds us that we have an old brain – some people talk about this as the reptilian brain – and he tells children that this is our downstairs brain which jumps into action in emergencies to help us be ready to fight, flee, or freeze in a split second. Our newer brain region, or what he calls the upstairs brain, helps us make moral and ethical decisions. When we use our whole brain, we help these parts work together. He outlines ways in which you can help your kids to integrate information and emotions.

For example, let's say your daughter is very upset about the rules you have set for bedtime and the subject matter she can watch on TV. Tonight her focus is on not being allowed to watch an episode of a series on TV that everyone has been talking about. You have told her once that she is late for bed time, she continues to postpone going to bed, and is now whining in the doorway.

Instead of using the command and demand strategy that most of us were raised on, there is another way. First, it is important to *connect* with your child when she is upset. Sit or kneel down to her eye level and rub her shoulder or her back in circle, close to where the heart is located. Look into her eyes and using a nurturing calm voice say something like "Gosh, you sound upset." While still rubbing, with neutral expression say, "Sometimes it is just hard to get through tough times isn't it?" Reassure her: "I want you to know I love you very much and you are so special. Can you tell me what is going on?" Repeat what she says is the problem, then redirect or offer more reassurance if she moves toward doing the right thing.

This strategy of "reconnect and redirect" allows you to use both your right brain to sense what is going on emotionally with your daughter (sad, mad, fearful, confused, frustrated, etc.) and provide right brain soothing by safe body contact of rubbing her back in a circle around her heart. By hearing her feelings and how she is experiencing the distressful situation, you also reinforce that she is important to you. Through redirection if she is engaging in behaviors that are making things worse, depending on her age you can co-create a solution for what to do next.

Sometimes all it takes to relieve some of that distress is for her to feel heard and important to you. At other times, it takes more attention to the situation and your using the left side of your brain – that logical side – to think through suggestions to help. And that is the second strategy – to *redirect with the left*, so that instead of ignoring or using a harsh tone, you are thinking through what she needs to feel safe and secure so that she can get through the disappointment of not getting her way, while also abiding by the family's rules that are now based on healthy values.

Not all children know what they are feeling. If you are in therapy, most likely you are often asked how something makes you feel. It is important to learn about the basic emotions we are all born with. Interest, excitement, joy and enjoyment are the feel good ones – our body actually feels good when we experience them. The other emotions (startle, fear, distress, anger, disgust, confusion, shame, humiliation) don't feel so good physically. In fact, the body may give us a cue when that emotion is present. For example, when you get angry, your blood pressure may go up, heart rate rises, jaw may be tight and if you are like us, your stomach churns. The more you know about how you are feeling, the more you can make good decisions about what to do that will help the situation. For kids, Siegel and Goleman reminds us to name the emotion and talk about how it feels in the body in order to tame it. Siegel recommends using story-telling to calm distressing emotions (or to celebrate the good feeling ones). If you have little children, concepts like the right and left side of the brain are too difficult to comprehend, but grade school and older children understand that the right side of the brain is where our feelings get going, the left brain can help us put feelings into words, and the two sides can work together to help us plan what to do at the moment or in the future.

Another characteristic found in youngsters who do well is the ability to set reachable goals. Additionally, these children feel that they know who they are—they have a sense of self-worth and self-identity. These young people are able to talk to their parents about anything (including sex) and talk with them often. In fact, talking is encouraged in these families and the family members report feeling heard.

Finally these children know their family's values and can articulate them. Think about how much easier it is for a kid to set boundaries with other children when he knows why you value boundaries and he has practiced with you how to set and keep a boundary.

Because we are speaking about sexual issues, it is also important to mention what happens in sexually healthy families. Parents consider sexuality education as important as all other types of values-based education. Parents are "askable"—children feel safe in asking. Parents utilize "teachable" moments rather than waiting for children to ask questions. They are aware that actions speak louder than words. Parents in these families know the difference between childhood and adult sexuality. Are you prepared to do these things?

Children in sexually healthy families feel good about their bodies, and understand the concept of privacy with regard to boundaries. They are prepared for puberty and feel comfortable asking their parents questions. They are able to make age-appropriate decisions.

So what does this have to do with disclosing to your children? This forms the foundation by which you will continue to talk about sexuality in your family. Disclosure to children means that your mate assumes responsibility for how his sexual acting out, drug abuse or addiction, compulsive gambling or other addictions, and you how your codependent behaviors or trauma reactivity have interfered with parenting your children. The discussions that follow are critical to rebuilding family and to help your child grow up thinking in a healthier way than you did about sexual and other behaviors.

Basic Repair Work

In preparing for your mate to disclose, here is what you need to do:

1. Discuss with your mate what information you both think needs to remain private between you as adults and marriage partners. (Some information may be okay for adult children to hear.) If it is not information that is crucial for children in order to make sound decisions about their own lives, then it can remain private between the two of you. Discuss with your mate the differences between the old values each of you were living by and the new ones that are driving your decisions now. Make a list of those together so you are both working from same value system. If you are alone and the addict is refusing to disclose, then you have to decide, based on your new values in recovery, what will be helpful for them to hear. Perhaps your sponsor or another peer will give you feedback on what values you are working under and how that influences what you will say.

2. Even though this is a disclosure about the addict's behavior, prepare to admit where you think you made mistakes along the way and encourage your child to talk about how she feels about what has been said. (To keep the communication flowing, let her know that she can think about it, write you a letter, or draw you a picture about how she feels.)

3. Both parents should be present and in agreement about what is going to be shared. Because it is a highly emotionally charged time for most people, it is safer for children to see both parents being involved in the process. *But the addict is responsible for disclosing his behavior.* (Partners often are aware that at times their behavior has been hurtful to the children too. The same process works, just at a different time.) Again, if the addict is not being responsible, then moving forward is important. In the spirit of keeping no secrets, letting your mate (the addict) know that you plan to disclose, what you plan to say, and give

him or her chance for input keeps you honest and less likely to do something in vindictive way, which only hurts the children.

4. Ask your child what she has heard or already knows and if she has any questions.

5. Remind him that he is free to ask you questions, and that you understand that this is hard for some people to talk about, so you are going to bring it up again from time to time.

Other Ongoing Repair Work

- Look for moments that are teachable opportunities—for example, a cybersex story on TV, cigarette use by young people or adults in a movie, or when someone gets arrested for prostitution.

- Focus more on the positive part of recovery—everyone working to have a balanced life.

- Spend time doing fun things together, to balance the "heavy" conversations you're having with your children. Children (especially early in your recovery) need fun time, too.

- If your child is angry and wants time apart from you or your mate, give him some space. However, do not forget the job of a parent is to provide structure and guidance. Encouraging your child to write you a letter about his anger is appropriate. Letting him hit you or allowing him to ignore house rules just because you didn't follow them is not okay. If the anger persists, and "connect and redirect" aren't working, then family therapy is in order.

- Discuss more about healthy sexuality other rather than just rehashing the old information about the disclosure.

- Be available. Be patient. Be proud that you are making every effort to be a different kind of parent. It will be worth it.

Despite the problems between you, you and your mate will want to show your children a united front in the fight against addiction in the way you disclose to them and in discussions after the disclosure. If they see you together even though the addict has misbehaved, it can help them to feel less anxious about the future and your role with them.

If a separation or divorce is the best solution for you, then co-parent your children in ways that show them that people can end one type of relationship and transition to another that is still respectful. When parents end up separating, the losses for children are multiple, so their needs are compounded by grief, fear, anger, and sadness.

Disclosure is not just a matter of having one little talk and it's over. In our most recent research on relapse, the majority of those respondents unfortunately had not yet disclosed to their children. Adult children tell us it is a very important part of the healing process for them as well. Let the disclosure start an ongoing process requiring many discussions.

There will be many opportunities for you to have teachable moments, so brainstorm with others what you will do and say when issues come up with your children. You have to think through what you will do if you find your daughter on the Internet chatting with some guy several years older than she and you find out it is she who is trying to talk him into meeting for sex. Or what you will do if you find printed pornography, pornography saved, or sites visited on your child's computer or phone, or if you walk into your twelve-year-old's room with a stack of laundry and find him or her masturbating. Or how you will handle watching a television program with your seven-year-old if a female character makes a sexually aggressive comment to a male. Yes, disclosure is but the first of many opportunities to talk about sexual health, drug use and abuse, healthy relationships, and developing into a responsible, authentic person. Your job is to keep coming back, offering to talk, listening, writing notes, being there for serious and fun times—*but be there*. Children of all ages need parental involvement and supervision. Be as genuine as possible. Don't lose your sense of humor. Have integrity about what you say and do with your children and you can survive almost anything.

Disclosure and discussing addiction are serious business, so limit the time you spend talking about the disease and expand the time you spend with your children talking about what they want to discuss, having fun, and having a positive attitude about the future.

References

Anda, Robert et al. The enduring effects of abuse and related adverse experiences in childhood. *European Archives of Psychiatry & Clinical Neuroscience*, 2006.

Carnes, Patrick. *The Betrayal Bond: Breaking Free of Exploitive Relationships*. Deerfield Beach, Fla.: Health Communications, Inc, 1997.

Carnes, Patrick. *Out of the Shadows*. New York: Bantam, 1991.

Corley, M. Deborah and Schneider, Jennifer. Sex addiction disclosure to children: The Parents' perspective. *Sexual Addiction & Compulsivity* 10:291-324, 2003.

Earle, Ralph & Earle. Marcus. *Sex Addiction: Case Studies and Management*. New York: Brunner Mazel, 1995.

Fongay, P. et al. Attachment, borderline states and the representation of emotion and cognition in self and other. In D. Cicchetti, S. L Toth, et al. (Eds.), *Emotions, cognition, and presentation* (pp. 371–414). Rochester, NY: University of Rochester Press, 1995.

Fossum, Merle & Marilyn Mason. *Facing Shame: Families in Recovery*. New York: Norton, 1986.

Goleman, Daniel. *Emotional Intelligence*. New York: Bantam, 1994.

Haffner, Debra. *From Diaper to Dating: A Parent's Guide to Raising Sexually Healthy Children*. New York: Newmarket Press, 1999.

Laaser, Mark. *Healing the Wounds of Sexual Addiction*. Grand Rapids, Mich.: Zondervan Publishing, 2004.

Siegel, Daniel. *The Developing Mind: Toward a Neurobiology of Interpersonal Experience*. New York: Guilford Press, 1999.

Siegel, Daniel. *The Whole-Brain Child: Revolutionary Strategies to Nurture Your Child's Developing Mind*. New York: Delacorte Press. 2011

Chapter Seven
The Other Disclosures

Previous chapters have described secrets, lies, and the initial disclosures involving interactions between a married or committed couple. But this is not the only kind of secret keeping that you may have to face. This chapter describes several real-life situations in which people have to decide whether to keep information private and hold a secret or to reveal it, and, if the latter, to whom. Let's begin with the story of the Malik family –Michael, his wife Martha, and their daughter Marjorie. Michael's cybersex addiction affected his entire family:

Martha, a 36-year old ICU nurse, had been married to Michael for 15 years. Early in their marriage a crisis ensued after Michael had spent too much money on pornographic magazines. He had thrown out the collection and promised Martha to reform. Since then, Martha suspected that Michael's habit had not disappeared, and kept an eye out for pornography in their home. After a few years she had relaxed, because she had not found any unaccounted for purchases nor magazines in the home.

Recently, however, Martha had noticed that Michael seemed to be withdrawing from the family. He spent hours holed up in his study at night, after explaining to her that he was working on a major computer project and needed to spend more time on it at home. Martha had noticed that Michael's interest in sex with her had diminished, but he explained that it was because he was working so hard and was too tired.

Martha's job, too, was very demanding, and the combination of a difficult job plus Michael's emotional absence began to take its toll on her, so that she became quite depressed. Even worse, Martha noticed that thirteen-year-old Marjorie had changed too. Formerly they'd had a close relationship, but now Marjorie seemed to be avoiding Martha. Marjorie also seemed angry with her father, occasionally even shouting at him. Martha's friends reassured her that it's common for teenagers to withdraw from their parents – it's a normal stage in their maturing process. But Martha's gut kept telling her that there must be some reason their family seemed to be falling apart.

In fact, there was a definite reason for what was happening. What Martha did not know was that Michael's nights were spent viewing online pornography, engaging in sex talk with other women in chat rooms, and having real-time sex with women online using video streaming. Marjorie had accidentally found him doing this one evening and was appalled. As Michael rearranged his clothing and flipped off the computer screen, Marjorie yelled that she was going to get her mother. Michael reminded Marjorie of how depressed her mother had been recently and implored her to keep the secret, for to tell would only hurt Martha. He told Marjorie that revealing the secret might result in breakup of the family, or even in a suicide attempt by Martha. In the end, he swore her to secrecy and promised to stop the activity. Marjorie's changed behavior was her attempt to keep the secret.

As we mentioned in Chapter 6, a situation like this puts the child in an impossible loyalty conflict for which there seems to be no way out. It guarantees that the child will feel guilty towards the unknowing parent. Her relationship with her father and siblings will also be altered – she is now in a position to blackmail her father in various ways and will also now feel a barrier between herself and her siblings, from whom she also has to keep the secret. To ask a child to hold a major secret from a parent is to do the child a grave disservice.

Learning about a person's sexual secrets from a child – or for that matter from any other source than the person – without a doubt increases the betrayal that a partner feels. Michael's best defense when he was about to be "outed," would have been to promptly disclose the secret himself, despite the inevitable initial trauma. His effort to persuade his daughter Marjorie to collude with him in keeping the secret from his wife is the worst possible thing he could have done. First, he has put his daughter in an impossible situation, causing harm that may require future therapy to undo. Marjorie is now in a double bind–by doing what she believes is best for one of her parents, she is being disloyal to the other. Whichever choice she makes, she will be hurting one of her parents. In addition, Michael has undermined his ability to be an effective parent to Marjorie, who is now in a position to pressure him to get preferential treatment compared to her siblings. Depending on her personality, Marjorie may feel a loss of respect for her mother and a sense of superiority to her, since she is now in possession of information that her mother doesn't have. When Martha eventually learns, as she is likely to, of both the cybersex behavior and of the cover-up effort involving daughter Marjorie, she is likely to be so angry that reconciliation may be impossible.

In addition to problems involving children and secrets, another difficult scenario is the initially incomplete disclosure that results in sequential or staggered revelations. This situation, usually due to an effort to evade the consequences of one's behaviors, was discussed in detail in Chapter 3. As our research has shown, the best outcome results when the addict provides full disclosure, in broad strokes rather than excruciating detail of all his addictive behaviors. In the long run, omitting a significant part of the acting out will only make things worse.

Several other situations involving secret keeping will be discussed in this chapter. These include:

- When a slip or relapse has occurred, so that additional disclosure is necessary

- When one member of a couple has acquired a sexually transmitted disease/infection or health problem due to addict's sharing dirty needles

- When one partner has already decided to leave

- When long-ago secrets have not been revealed; timing of disclosure

- When the secret involves a friend, neighbor, or colleague.

- When the parent is not the biological parent.

- When your mate is gay or lesbian

In this chapter we will discuss good and bad ways of handing the above situations.

Learning About Your Mate's Relapse

Sometimes staggered or sequential disclosures occur, not because the addict is deliberately hiding some information or has forgotten some events, but rather because he has experienced a slip or relapse and now has new secrets to uncover, new lies to reveal to you.

As mentioned in Chapter 5, we recommend that at the time of the first disclosure you discuss with your mate how much information you want to hear. After you and the addict work through the initial revelations, you need to determine what information you want on an ongoing basis. Some partners want to know when someone has a slip and what the addict is doing to get his recovery back in line. Others want the addict to take that information to his or her sponsor or therapist, but do want to know if the addicted person has relapsed in ways that will harm the partner. Because slips and relapses are a common part of any addiction, it is very helpful to have this discussion in advance.

Unfortunately, the partner is often so in shock or angry and hurt that it takes a while to get clear about what to share. Revisiting several times during first couple of years of recovery what you want to be told is important.

It is not easy to be honest in this situation. Perhaps you have told your mate, "If you ever use again, you're history." Or perhaps your mate has spent months trying to rebuild trust, and he may believe that learning about his slip or relapse will set your level of trust back to zero. Perhaps he feels so much shame at his "failure" that he cannot bring himself to confess what happened.

Understand that this is a common experience. In our most recent research on disclosure of relapse (Corley, Schneider & Hook, 2012), we found that over 75% of the addicts reported they had experienced multiple relapses. When relapse happens, a decision about a new disclosure must be made. Below are the reactions of several spouses to hearing about a mate's relapse:

A woman who decided to stay with her husband after he had another affair wrote,

> *I was very upset. He had had such great sobriety. I thought we had beaten his addiction and that it was 'history.' I shared about*

the effects of the relapse on me at my COSA meetings and had other people to talk to. I knew the behavior was about him, not me, but still I was really disappointed. We had been separated for two years while he was acting out, but this time I didn't even consider another separation. We wouldn't put our son through that again. As I saw it, we could each continue working on our individual recovery, or we could divorce if we felt there was nothing to work on.

Another woman reported she has learned a lot from her husband's relapses:

When my husband had his first relapse just after his first birthday in the program, I was totally shocked; he was one of the stars of the program. I was angry, hurt, and scared. When three months later there was another relapse, I wasn't very shocked, and experienced much less anger. The second time I didn't process as much anger with him – instead I processed with COSA and Al-Anon people and in my journal. I have grown a tremendous amount as a result of the two relapses. I have moved from dependence on him to dependence on myself and on being a 'big' person.

Yet another woman is considering divorce after learning of several relapses:

When I finally was told the truth about his relapse I chose to accept that as an addict, he fell off the wagon, just like taking one more drink or drug. That allowed me to be at peace and accepting of him. After two years and two more relapses, I realize that this is a process and that nothing is black or white. I am, though, at a point in my life where my tolerance for "gray" has worn as thin as it can. I am considering divorce.

In each of the cases above, the spouse was knowledgeable about the disease of addiction and aware that relapse is always a possibility. Each spouse had had experience with a Twelve-Step program for information and support. Each one was able to separate the addict's behavior from herself and not "take it personally," and could rationally consider her choices rather than respond out of neediness and fear of being alone. In the last case, because the relapses were continuing, the wife was considering an end to the marriage.

The partner's response might have been very different if she were not herself in recovery and if she did not understand the nature of addictive disorders and the need to detach from the behaviors. In such a situation, her fear might be greater and her tolerance for a less-than-perfect recovery greater. She would most likely had believed that the addict's problem had been "cured" and would be less likely to accept the relapsing nature of the disorder.

A relapse involving another person is likely to be more threatening to the partner and to be considered a more serious betrayal than is behavior involving only the addict. For example, if a sex addict masturbated or accessed pornography on the Internet instead of using a prostitute, learning about it would be less threatening to a partner. Or if an alcoholic left the bar after one drink rather than getting drunk and driving drunk with his children in the car, the partner would be more able to view the relapse as less serious.

In our research on relapse we found it makes a significant difference in how partners view the addict and the relationship if their mate revealed the slip or relapse before they discovered it. In fact, in those couples where the addict disclosed, they reported significantly more satisfaction with the relationship, were emotionally closer, had a more satisfying sexual relationship and reported higher levels of trust than did the couples in which the partner discovered the relapse. That is why we recommend, that as hard as it is to face a serious slip or relapse, it is better for the addict to talk about what to do if (or when) it happens.

There are several factors which will contribute to a favorable outcome of your mate's disclosure of a relapse.

1. The addict's commitment to making changes that will contribute to ongoing sobriety. These can include increasing his Twelve-Step involvement, reconnecting with or getting a new sponsor, making his environment safer, beginning or resuming therapy. You are likely to have a more positive and understanding reaction to your mate's disclosure if he is taking steps to learn from the relapse and prevent it from happening again. If he has made *no* changes, then he needs to identify the changes he needs to make and start making those immediately.

2. Letting you know the exact nature of the slip. He may even want to do what is called a "relapse autopsy." This is where he not only describes exactly what happened, but also identifies everything that contributed to the "death" of his recovery efforts. Did he identify the triggers that occurred? Was he in such an emotional situation in a high-risk environment so he thought it "just happened" before he was even aware that he was acting out? Did he make seemingly unimportant decisions that contributed to getting in that wrong environment? Did his acting out put you at risk of a sexually transmitted disease or other adverse consequences? If he is continuing to put you in harm's way with the knowledge he has about addiction and recovery, then the problem needs to be addressed more seriously

3. Your involvement in your own recovery program and/or in counseling is just as important as his care. A partner who is not working on herself is likely to be more frightened of a slip or relapse, more likely to continue perceiving herself as a victim, and less likely to be empathetic to the addict's struggles. Sometimes when the partner has not been in a recovery program herself, she remains caught in her anger and resentment. Some partners have an anxious attachment style, and fear intimacy; these style of attachment can use the addict's behavior as a way to obtain distance and derive energy from the drama. The partner with this style of attachment does not do well when hearing about slips, much less relapses. The information becomes fuel for the fire of anger. In such a case, it would be helpful for the addict to come cleanwithin a therapy session.

4. Do you and your mate have a supportive environment in which to carry out the disclosure? The ideal setting is in a therapy session, after your mate has had a chance to discuss the relapse with the therapist. Twelve-Step sponsors, or another couple in recovery, are other possible resources.

5. You and your mate need to decide what information will be helpful to you to have, and what is better for the addict to share with another support system. Revealing all slips is not always in the best interest of the relationship. You might prefer only to know the steps the addict is taking to make changes in thoughts and actions.

He or She Exposed Me to a Health Risk. What Now?

Most of the time the addict has some time to consider exactly when and how to reveal painful information to the partner. However, in certain cases the outcome can be much worse if he does not tell immediately. One such situation was discussed above – if your child, a friend, or the law has information that they are likely to reveal to you soon. Our research has shown that if partners learn about the behavior directly from the addict rather than from someone else, they are much more likely to get past their initial reaction more quickly and to work constructively with the addict on resolving the problem.

Another situation requiring urgent action is when the addict has caught or possibly been infected with a virus or other infection as a result of unprotected sexual interactions or sharing needles. (Any activity with another person that involves sharing even the smallest quantity of bodily fluid can be the entrance route of a virus or other infection.) Not all infections show symptoms immediately, so the longer the addict waits to disclose to you, the longer he is putting both of you at risk. You may need to visit a doctor for evaluation and possible treatment. At the very least, your mate will need to begin using condoms or to abstain from sex or other activities with you that might spread the infection to you. In both cases, you obviously need an explanation and the sooner the better. We know of several partners who chose to leave the marriage because they felt that the single biggest betrayal they'd experienced was that their mate continued to expose them to health risks. One of them told us,

> He had shared needles and had unprotected sex with other men, and then he'd have sex with me. We have two young children. He put his own pleasure above my life and potentially, that of our children! He was willing to expose me to a fatal disease. When I finally found out, all I wanted to do was put as much distance as possible between us. We are now divorced. Thank heavens I didn't catch anything from him.

Partners recognize sooner or later that it is painful and risky for the addict to admit to you that you are at risk for an STD or other health problem, and that doing this shows caring. On the flip side, the message a partner gets when the addict repeatedly exposes her to HIV, hepatitis, chlamydia and other diseases is that he just doesn't care. Postponing this disclosure makes it far more likely that the eventual outcome will be the end of the relationship.

When Long-ago Secrets Have Not Been Revealed

Jay had been in recovery from his sex addiction for two years when he and Monica had dinner out with friends one evening. In a conversation about "the old days," Jay recalled how three years earlier, he and Monica had had a fight and she backed out of accompanying him out of town on a business trip. Upset with her, he'd phoned a stripper to visit him in his hotel room. Monica clearly remembered what Jay had told her at the time to explain the charge on his credit card, and she now chimed into the conversation: "and when he actually saw the stripper, she was so unattractive that Jay paid her and sent her away." Jay looked at her as though she must be insane.

"I would never have done that!" He readily admitted that they'd had sex. Monica was livid. Once they were alone in the parking lot, she angrily confronted him.

"You lied to me! You told me you'd sent her away! How could you have done this? How can I ever trust you?"

Jay sighed and looked at her wearily, "Monica, before I got into recovery I told you so many lies that I no longer remember exactly what I said. Lying was so much a part of my life back then that I lied even when I didn't have to. I'm sorry about this particular lie, but I'm sure that there will be other occasions when you will realize I lied in the past. All I can say is I haven't lied to you once since I got into recovery two years ago, and I intend to continue being honest with you. That's the best I can say."

Monica realized that what he said made sense, and that she would have to accept the possibility of other lies without getting upset all over again. For two years Jay had given her no reason to doubt his word. She would have to draw a line between the "bad old days" and the time in recovery, and judge them differently. She would have to forgive the past, meaning to be able to hear about it without getting upset all over again. Part of the task of doing this turned out to be a period of grieving the loss of the past as she had previously perceived it. Instead, she had to accept that her life with Jay had been a web of lies and deceptions, not the great marriage she thought she had.

Additionally, Monica might have asked Jay to be more sensitive with information from the past or perhaps set a boundary with Jay about not bringing up past acting out behaviors until they had talked about them in private.

When a Parent is Not the Biological Parent

Another situation involves a long-ago secret kept from a child. One such dilemma was described in a column in a 2011 column in the New York Times "The Ethicist."

A man wrote,

> I didn't find out for years, but I fathered a child with a woman who was, and still is, married to another man. The girl does not know any of this. Neither does the husband. At the mother's request, I have had nothing to do with the girl. . . Does the girl have a right to know her true parentage upon reaching adulthood? Sooner? Over the objection of the mother? Only when the husband dies? Who can make these decisions and when?

The columnist's reply was that such information could have devastating consequences for the entire family – or the outcome could be very good, explaining to the girl some clues she may have long perceived. The mother is the person in the best position to evaluate the best option, and her judgment should not be overruled. "If you feel strongly that the girl should know, talk to her mother and try to reach a consensus – a consensus that would eventually, if painfully, have to include the woman's husband."

Recent research on adopted children and those born as a result of donated sperm and/or eggs has shown that such children very often want information about their biological parents or egg or sperm donor. They are very curious about where they came from. Professional organizations such as the American Society for Reproductive Medicine, and adoption agencies now recommend disclosing to children, most commonly before puberty. Some European countries no longer permit anonymous gamete donations. But when the child's conception involved secrecy and betrayal on the part of one parent, then there are obviously complex issues to be resolved around making this decision.

When the Secret Involves a Neighbor or Friend

Susan lives in a subdivision consisting of many homes with the same floor plan. One day she notices that her next-door neighbor Ike is peeping into the bedroom window of another neighbor across the street. She thinks this is odd, but soon forgets about it. A few days later she again sees Ike standing outside the neighbor's bedroom window. Should Susan confront Ike? Tell Ike's wife? Call the police? Tell the neighbor who'd been spied on?

Again, there are no clear-cut answers. Susan's decision is likely to be influenced by her relationship with the people involved. She may decide to have no direct contact with the neighbors but rather only to call the police. After all, it's not her responsibility to tell the wife. The wife might not appreciate another woman calling her and telling her that her husband is a voyeur. She might become angry and threatening, and might blame the messenger. The police might interview the man, which would certainly catch his attention and make it more likely he will get help. Even if the police don't do anything, they will have a record of the incident in case they are notified that he was caught in another voyeuristic act.

Susan might decide to tell the police, and also to tell the voyeur, advising him to tell his wife before the police do. Susan might instead notify the wife, believing that she is the one who has the most leverage and is most likely to be able to pressure him into treatment. Also, the wife might want to be told – this might not be the first time, and she may already be aware of the behavior or suspects it. (Of course, the wife may well be aware of the voyeur's activities and has had no luck in getting him to get help).Moreover, if the police are involved, and the man arrested, it could well have adverse consequences for the wife and children, so better to begin by telling the wife. Whether or not to speak to the man's wife would depend on the relationship between the two women. If they were friends, the wife would more likely want Susan to alert her to the situation if she were not already aware of it.

Finally, Susan might decide to notify the neighbor who had been spied on, on the grounds that the neighbor had been the victim and needs to know so she can decide whether to notify the police as well as how to protect herself in the future.

Once again, there is often no one right answer. No wonder it is difficult for the average person to decide what to disclose, how much, to whom, and when!

When You Learn that a Friend's Spouse is Having an Affair, Using Drugs, or Gambling Compulsively

A closely related and more common ethical dilemma is what to do if you learn that the spouse of your close friend is having an affair or any other addictive behavior. Do you tell your close friend? The late Dr. Shirley Glass, author of *NOT Just Friends*, a psychologist specializing in infidelity, related that she usually advises confronting the offending person first and advises the person to tell the partner; if not, then you will do it. The reason is that otherwise the friendship is ruined because it is too uncomfortable to be carrying those kinds of secrets. In her experience, Dr. Glass told us,

> "When the betrayed partner later found out that other people knew, they were very hurt and angry. In many cases, the relationships were permanently severed because they focused their feelings of betrayal on the colluder who could be a potential informant." (Personal Communication, May 28, 2001).

Interestingly, in Dr. Glass's experience, when someone does eventually tell the betrayed partner about the affair, it is most commonly the affair partner, who presumably wanted to drive a further wedge between her lover and his spouse. "It usually backfired because the crisis it evoked was a catalyst to stop the affair and rebuild the marriage."

We have known sex addicted women involved in affairs with married men who tell the wife as an external intervention for themselves. The sex addicted women knew that telling the wife would likely end the affair when the addict was not able to.

The stories in this chapter represent some real-life situations. The correct approach is not always clear; gray areas abound. As we have seen, determining the best course involves, above all, communication. If you are uncertain about whether to disclose or keep a secret, about whether telling will help or hurt your partner, your recovery, and/or your relationship, consult others. Talk with a sponsor, a counselor, or a friend. Sometimes the uncertainty remains. You may need to follow your heart and take the risk of opening your heart to your partner, even if the outcome is uncertain.

When Your Mate has Disclosed to You that he is Gay or she is Lesbian

Being told by your mate that he or she has been sexual with other people is difficult for any partner, but learning that the reason is his sexual orientation provides an additional challenge. Many straight partners have some suspicion that their mate is gay or has same-sex attraction; others don't know. No matter what is known, often partners react to the disclosure with shock, confusion, fear, anger, and sadness. Feeling sexually desired by their mates is a normal expectation for women. It is also normal that they feel a blow to their feminine sexuality when they are told by their husband that he wants or needs something sexually that women cannot give him. No matter how positive their self-esteem is, they are initially likely to feel devalued. One wife said,

> *If it was another woman I probably would have thought I just have to compete better. I could be sexier, wear different clothes, or do more. But how do you compete with a man? What they really want, you can't give them. It was like a total repudiation of my womanhood. I used to love the pride I had within myself as a woman, being attractive to the man I chose to marry. Now I don't have that.*

On the other hand, another wife had a different perspective. She wrote,

> *If my husband had sex with another woman, I would be much more upset than I am now, because I would take that as a very personal affront. It would tell me that I am inadequate. I know I can't give him what a man can.*

But the revelation that your mate is gay has wider implications than what happens in the bedroom: It often portends the doom of the marriage. Because of the stigma that has been associated with homosexuality, it is logical that gays and lesbians would decide that marrying a straight partner would be the answer. Some hope that this straight marriage will "cure" their attraction and desire to be with a same-gender partners. Others just want a cover and believe they can lead a secret life without hurting anyone. Many fall in love with their straight partners, have children, and live the life that they believe is expected of them – for a while, but then the emotional distress and desire for a same-sex partner comes back and for most, over time gets worse.

By the time they tell their partner, some gays and lesbians have already decided to leave the marriage. If your mate hasn't decided, or else wants to stay, then you will need to figure out if you want to stay married, or work out some other arrangement, especially if you have children. All this will take time, after you have gone through the initial reactions to the disclosure. At first, some partners feel a sense of relief because there have been sexual problems in the relationship and now they know why; others want to continue the marriage and to continue enjoying the emotional connection, but no longer want to be sexual. Some just don't understand what happened, end up blaming themselves, and want to try some other kind of therapy to save the marriage. Some are bitter and feel betrayed but insist on staying married out of confusion, spite, fear of being alone, or for financial or health reasons.

Amity Pierce Buxton, author of *Other Side of the Closet: The Coming Out Crisis for Straight Spouses* (1994) reports that many partners become depressed and isolated, are too embarrassed to tell friends or family members, and have little knowledge of how to get support. An excellent website for partners is the Straight Spouse Network (www.ssnetwk.org). It provides many resources including answers to many questions partners have and support group websites in many communities. We also strongly recommend that you find a therapist to provide you with support and help you decide what to do.

When You or Your Spouse Really Wants to Leave

After years of struggling in his troubled marriage, 50-year old Arthur was ready to call it quits with Angie. He progressively distanced himself emotionally, and finally got involved in an affair with a younger woman he'd met at the company where he was doing some consulting work.

Perhaps on some level Arthur wanted Angie to find out; perhaps he was hoping that if she caught him, Angie would demand a divorce, so that he wouldn't have to take the initiative himself. At any rate, he left enough clues around that it didn't take Angie long to figure out what was happening.

Her response, however, was not what he'd been expecting. Instead of announcing the end of the marriage, Angie took all the blame on herself and insisted on going to counseling to try to save the relationship. Not wanting to hurt her even more, Arthur couldn't face telling Angie directly that he wanted to leave, so he reluctantly assented to joint counseling.

In preliminary individual sessions, the counselor learned that Arthur had emotionally left the marriage years earlier. He explained to Arthur that couple counseling is likely to be effective only if both partners have the same goal. In Arthur's case, he was only prolonging and postponing the pain that Angie would inevitably feel at learning the truth. The counselor persuaded Arthur to reveal to Angie in a joint session that, for him, the marriage was irretrievably broken.

Acknowledging a painful secret can be made less painful for the recipient if it is accompanied by a declaration of a commitment to the relationship. If you and your mate have a long history together, have had memories of many good times, and perhaps children, it may be very difficult to admit that the marriage has ended for you, especially if you believe that this will be devastating for everyone.

As we will see in Chapter 9, however, for those who whose marriage ends, there is life after divorce, even for the one who still feels committed to the marriage. Although at first, life without your mate may indeed seem to be hardly worth living, but soon enough you will reclaim yourself and realize that life has much to offer. People who are in a Twelve-Step recovery program can call on the support of their program friends, a counselor, and the tools of the program and can indeed become contented and fulfilled. While we do caution against acting too quickly regarding the future of a marriage after a disclosure, if your marriage has been over for some time, tell your mate and then begin to heal from the loss.

References

Buxton, Amity Pierce, *Other Side of the Closet: The Coming Out Crisis for Straight Spouses*. New York: Wiley (1994)

Corley, M Deborah, Schneider, Jennifer P. and Hook, Joshua. Partners' decision-making after disclosure of sex addiction relapse. *Sexual Addiction & Compulsivity*, 2012, in press.

Chapter Eight
Special Issues

Your partner's disclosure to you and your children is extremely difficult for everyone involved. The addict who comes clean usually experiences an immediate sense of relief. The experiences for the partner and children, however, are varied. Matters are further complicated when you (and of course the addict too) have to decide what to say at work, with family members and friends, or within your faith community.

Family Members

Depending on your relationship with your parents, siblings, and other extended family members, most addicts and partners want family members to have some information. If you are estranged from family members, then you may decide to keep private the information about your mate's addiction. However, if family members provide emotional support for you, it is important that they have general knowledge of what is going on in your life. There may be other members of your family who are dealing with similar problems or have dealt with them and can be of help to you cope with your situation. Some partners can identify generations of other family members who have struggled with addictions:

> I recently found out from my Dad that he was involved with other women in the course of his marriage. One of them was my mom's best friend and they did some things like spouse swapping. He didn't tell me anything about my Mom's activities, only that he thought that since Arthur and I were having problems in our marriage, it might be helpful for us to know that he'd had some problems in that area too. But the implication was that maybe my Mom had done a lot of that too, playing around with other men. I had some indication of it on some level, that something was wrong which I didn't want to look at too closely, and maybe that's why I don't remember much about my childhood.

Being exposed to addictive behavior happens in a variety of ways. The wife of a sex addict reported,

> *My father never physically molested me, but he was verbally sexual with me. He'd make dirty jokes about my body. At times I'd be in the bathroom putting on makeup and he'd come in and urinate and walk around naked. I was disgusted by him. I had one aunt who was very pretty and well endowed, and at one party I saw him feeling her. I still remember the disgust I felt. I felt very sorry for my mother, and at the same time angry with her. My father used to keep Playboy magazines in the house, so I grew up looking at pornography and reading all the books he had.*
>
> *I also think my father had affairs. One day when I was in the house and my father was outside washing the car, the phone rang. It was a woman who said she wanted my dad. I asked, "Who's this?" She answered, "It's Baby." So I went out the back door and called, "Dad, there's a woman on the phone and she says her name is Baby." My father turned white and proceeded to have a heart attack. I can still remember him walking into the house, clutching his chest, and then the ambulance coming. I thought it was my fault, and I went around for years feeling guilty for causing his heart attack.*
>
> *I felt so lonely all my life, so I tried to find companionship by having boyfriends. By sixth grade I was kissing and petting because it gave me the feeling that the boys cared about me. If someone wasn't being sexual with me, they didn't care about me. All through high school I had boyfriend after boyfriend.*

The same principles apply for telling close family members as do for telling partners. Provide only general information that may be educational as well, but leave out the details. You may have identified ways in which your attempts to cope with the addict's behavior may have hurt your children and other family members; It is also helpful at this juncture to apologize to them. You and your mate need to decide what he and you will reveal and what you want to keep private between the two of you. The addict should acknowledge his behavior and addiction, you about your behavior and addictions, if applicable.

SPECIAL ISSUES

In the box is a sample of what your mate might write or say about his behavior to parents or parents-in-law who are supportive and with whom you or he feel close:

> Dad and Mom:
>
> I want to thank you for meeting me. What I have to say is very important and it is important to me that you are willing to do this. The purpose of this meeting is not to blame anyone for anything—what I have done is my responsibility alone. My purpose is to let you know what has been going on with me and Susan and what I plan to do about it.
>
> You may not know that Susan and I have been having problems. We are pretty good at keeping secrets. I have been very good at keeping secrets, not only from Susan, but from everyone.
>
> For many years I have been using sex like a drug—like a drug addict would, to make me feel better when I feel anxious, or depressed, sad, or mad. Sometimes I use it when I feel good because I don't know how to deal with feeling good either. The point is, I don't know how to handle how I feel and I learned early in life that one way to do it is through a sexual release. Some people call this sex addiction, so I now call myself a sex addict.
>
> I don't want to tell you all the details of what I do because that is something I deal with in therapy and with Susan. I am also in a Twelve-Step program much like Alcoholics Anonymous and it is helping me learn how to handle my feelings. In therapy I am learning more how to have confidence in myself, and Susan and I are working on how to be healthy together.
>
> I want to say again, I am not blaming my parents or anyone for how I am. Lots of people hear that someone becomes a sex addict because of something that happened in their childhood. I have come to believe that lots of things from my childhood influenced how I saw the world and responded to it, but now I am an adult and can make adult choices in responsible ways. I am grateful to you for all you have done for me.

> There are lots of books you can read to find out more about sex addiction. I can recommend a few and I am willing to answer some questions. The only questions I won't respond to are those that Susan and I want to keep between us.
>
> I need your support and love now. I am sorry for the hardship this has caused everyone involved and for the worry I have caused you. I am better and have great hope for the future.
>
> I love you.
>
> Your son, Al.

Then ask them—Do you have any questions now?

Many partners (just like many addicts) have been the victims of sexual trauma within their families of origin, and are in a delicate position with regard to disclosing about the addict's behavior and about what they have learned about their own history. However, disclosure can provide freedom from shame and help a survivor move forward in his/her recovery. If you, the partner, are a survivor of sexual trauma, you may at some point be ready to discuss this with your parents. Before you do, you may want to talk with your therapist about how to handle resolution of those issues as part of your healing process. If those issues have been addressed in your family of origin and you feel safe within that family system, a discussion with your family is appropriate. Ending the family secrets is an important step to stopping the multigenerational transmission of these traits.

Often survivors are tempted to blame parents for the sexual abuse the survivor endured. It is important to obtain therapy for childhood sexual trauma. Remember, *the therapy for holding the victimizer accountable is different from disclosure. Disclosure is important in order for you to be accountable for your behavior.* It is appropriate, nonetheless, for survivors to include, as part of their disclosure, the boundaries they need to make public. An example is shown in the next box:

Dad:

The purpose of this letter and our meeting is for me to explain what I have been doing that is very unhealthy for me. I also want to talk about what I have learned about myself in therapy, what I am doing to help myself, and what I would like you to do to help me with this.

I learned early in my life that sex is the most important sign of love, that I could control men through sex, and that it was my job to take care of a man. I needed a man to make me feel worthwhile. This may be related to the sexual interactions between you and me, but I am not blaming you for my behavior. I am responsible for what I have done and the choices I have made. I repeatedly made bad choices in men, picking people who it turned out had serious problems such as alcoholism or sex addiction, whom I thought I could help. In my marriage, I spent too much time worrying about Bob and not enough time being a good mom to the kids. But I am doing better now. I am going to Twelve Step meetings, therapy, Bob and I are going to therapy, and are getting along better, and I am learning to be a better mom.

To help me with my recovery, I have a couple of requests. First, when we are together, I need to have more space. I get anxious when you want to put your arms around me all the time. I also get uncomfortable when you talk about your girlfriends and about having sex with them. I'd like us to focus on talking about the kids, work, the weather, movies, or things like that. If you have some problem with me, then it is okay to tell me about it and I will do the same with you. Then we both can make decisions like adults about what to do next. In the past, I've made matters worse when we disagreed by yelling at you and then at my kids. For now, I'd like no touching until we are about to leave, then a brief hug is okay.

I appreciate that you have listened and that you came to talk to me today. Do you have any questions?

Setting boundaries to help you maintain your recovery is important. This is an appropriate time for the survivor to do it.

A New Love Relationship: When your Partner is an Addict

When a man or woman seeks a new relationship, they will naturally put their best foot forward. As you peruse the prospects on a dating site such as match.com, you will read about their education, interests, career, tri-weekly attendance at the gym, and the places they have visited. You will not find information about anyone's addiction history or psychiatric problems. Addicts and people with medical (e.g. Herpes) or psychiatric problems inevitably face a challenge about when to inform the new person in their life about these difficult realities. All addicts are at risk for relapse, no matter how long they have been sober. Informing a potential mate is important. But when to tell is determined by the type of addiction, any legal issues involved, and the seriousness of the relationship.

Many addicts say that they are not going to divulge their past until they are sure this person is "the one." Unfortunately this can backfire because a potential mate will take the delay as a lack of trust and, in some instances, a form of dishonesty that he did not open up before the relationship became serious. If your new love discloses to you later than you think he should have, recognize that this was a difficult decision on his part, because he did not want to lose you.

Most people are pretty accepting of drug addiction or gambling and food issues; people are less likely to respond positively and more likely to jump to conclusions when it comes to sex addiction. As your new relationship progresses and begins to get more serious, your new friend may initiate a conversation with you about the importance of telling each other the truth and not keeping secrets. He may tell you that the relationship has grown to a degree that he believes it is time to disclose information that for the most part is private in his life. Your initial reaction is likely to be anxiety or fear about what is coming next. Remember that he has probably spent many hours getting up the courage to initiate this talk, and wouldn't do it if he didn't care. Listen to him with an open mind. Here is the story of one woman who took the risk of disclosing in her new relationship.

SPECIAL ISSUES

Latoya was a gambling addict. Although she had abused alcohol and had smoked cigarettes for years, gambling was her main route to escape her feelings of inadequacy and her fear of her first husband's temper. She gambled in isolation and secrecy. Her first marriage had ended in divorce. It took her seven years to get her gambling under control and her finances back in order. Dating was long in coming. Eventually she met a man close to her age, Washington, who was also divorced and who had two children. Initially she accepted invitations to accompany Washington to church and then other activities which included his children. After Washington started to ask her to dinner and the movies without the children, Latoya was convinced that Washington was getting as serious as she felt. This is what she shared with him about her addiction:

Washington, I am so fond of you and your children. You have done such a wonderful job of raising them. I feel like our relationship is getting pretty serious and feel like I owe you much. Part of what I owe you is the truth about me. If we are going to have some type of commitment to each other in the future, I think you deserve to know this about me.

I am a gambling addict. That is why I go to meetings at the church on Wednesday and Saturdays—I go to meetings for my addiction then. I also used to drink heavily when I gambled, and I smoked. That is why I don't drink now and was attracted to you because you don't smoke. My first marriage was rough and I used gambling to escape my feelings. I was not able to face my fear of my husband and in the end I only made him angrier because I forced us into such debt. Even after we divorced, when I had basically nothing, I stole money from him and continued to write checks on our old account. I was just lucky I did not get into trouble legally. I had to file bankruptcy and am just now beginning to get my credit reestablished.

I have seven years of solid recovery with no relapses, but I know as an addict I will never be totally free of this disease. That is why I still go to meetings after all these years—they help me stay grounded, help others, and remind me of where I have been. I hope this doesn't change things between us—you mean the world to me and I would hate for our friendship to end.

This disclosure had a happy ending. Washington appreciated Latoya's honesty and was encouraged by her long-term recovery. Latoya and Washington were married about a year later. Washington supports Latoya in her efforts to sponsor other addicts as well as tell her story in the church where they attend services.

Evelyn had a more difficult time after her fiancé George disclosed to her about his past behavior. She was very much in love with George, and had gladly accepted the beautiful 2-carat diamond engagement ring he gave her. But he kept postponing their wedding for over 2 years because – as she later found out – he was frightened of the consequences of disclosing to her. George had a history of pornography and masturbation, sexual contact with male masseurs, and unsafe sex with both men and women. Finally, after intensive individual therapy, Twelve-Step program, and medication for depression and intrusive thinking, he achieved a year of sobriety and became convinced he had to tell Evelyn.

Evelyn was shocked by George's disclosure. Despite their long courtship, this took her some time to get over. At first, she was very disturbed and angry about his acting out during their engagement. It took her several therapy sessions to clarify the impact this information had on her and the relationship. She was not as disturbed by the homosexual encounters as she was about the intercourse with a woman during their engagement. Evelyn reported being upset more by the secret keeping than anything else. Because of the infidelity in her first marriage she quickly concluded that this relationship would end the same way.

However, after she had had an opportunity to voice her anger at the betrayal, and have her feelings validated as normal, she began to have more compassion for George and how difficult the disease had been for him to manage. It helped her to know about addiction and she began to see his behavior as a result of the disease instead of thinking something was wrong with her. She gained hope from the full year of sobriety he had when he disclosed and began to understand that he had waited until he could actually report at least a year of recovery before he disclosed. Evelyn was grateful that George valued her enough to tell her before they were married so she could make an informed choice. She said if he had waited until after the wedding, she would have had the marriage annulled immediately. Through more couples counseling and a great deal of discussion with their priest, this couple was able to move ahead with their marriage plans within a year of the disclosure.

Not all partners can get past some disclosures, especially if the sexual acting out involved children, multiple partners, was ongoing for years, included unprotected sex followed by putting the partner at risk for HIV or other STDs, or behaviors that resulted in arrest. Even if these elements were not present, if there was a long history of repeated lying, partners may feel they could never trust the addict again. Over and over again partners report that repeated lying is one of the most likely reasons to leave a relationship. Disclosure is definitely taking a risk. But the longer the addict waits, the more likely he or she is to lose the partner.

Friends

Friends are a very important source of support to women. Sometimes it is easier to open up to close friends than to family. Some partners feel so much shame that they don't tell friends what's going on. They may fear that the friend will think it was the partner's fault that the addict acted out. However, in most cases, the partner discloses to the friend what she feels comfortable telling and uses the friendship as a means of support for her. Some partners unload all the details of the addict's behavior to the friend, who then aligns with the partner and becomes protective toward her and angry with the addict. If the couple remain together and eventually work through the problem, the partner's relationship with the friend may become strained, as the friend may continue to criticize the addict.

Be clear with your friend the role you want him or her to play. Your friend should be there to listen, reflect, and then ask questions or remind you of what you have said you want to do to change. If you want your friend to fight the battle for you, you will not learn.

Besides disclosing, tell your friend how he or she can help you. Be specific. Sometimes it is unclear to friends whether you are seeking support for leaving or you just want to vent. Let them know that venting helps you, but that you are not ready to give up the relationship with your mate (unless you are) and that all you need is for your friend to acknowledge what awareness you have gained and validate how difficult it is for you.

Disclosure After an Arrest

There are certain circumstances in which one is forced to decide how to handle situations when other people find out. This may be because an arrest is made and a sheriff or police officer comes to your home or place of work and arrests your mate. Sometimes notification of the arrest is printed in the newspaper. If the arrest seems newsworthy, the media may get involved. Each of these situations prompts worry and curiosity by family members, neighbors, and co-workers.

When legal cases have not been settled, often you and your mate have to tell those who are important to you that you cannot speak about the case per the attorney's advice, but that you need their support. Look for ways people can help—respite care for the children, cooking a meal, providing a shoulder to cry on.

Sometimes enough information is already public that you are forced to say something. If your mate's "case" has been publicized through the media, and they are approaching you, your family, or your neighbors, decide what you are going to say to the media with your mate and run it by his attorney. Frequently a "no comment" stance or "you can speak with my attorney" is useful. Providing your kids with a "no comment" answer is helpful. We are so tempted to give the media the true story, imagining that fair-minded people can make sense of your spouse's addiction and will quickly forgive him or be less angry with him. Unfortunately that is often not the case, at least in the beginning. In too many cases the media will distort the truth, omit crucial details, or slant the story in ways that will make you both regret you said anything.

But make it possible for your children to play with their playmates, providing them with language to use to talk about the situation. For example, a 6 to 8-year-old child might say to a friend, "Some people said that my Daddy did some bad stuff. I don't know what happened and I don't want to talk about it. I love my Daddy and I don't want to talk about it. OK? If you keep talking about it, I have to go home."

Be supportive of your mate and children but allow them opportunities to vent their feelings. Listen, acknowledge to the addict that you know this is a difficult time for him or agree that the media are not being fair or nice, and ask what you can do *today* to help him feel better. Even if your family members are not able to manage their own feelings during these times, manage your own emotional state in healthy ways. Vent your anger and sadness with friends with whom you can talk, with recovery peers if you yourself are in a recovery program, and with your therapist, and develop ways to stay focused on helping your family in these high stress times.

Telling Neighbors or Members of Your Faith Community

Once the court situation is over, depending on the age of your children and following the tips in Chapter 6, be prepared to help your mate disclose and then provide ongoing information to help your youngsters cope with the situation. Decide on a need-to-know basis what to tell specific neighbors and those outside your immediate circle of family and best friends. Discuss with your mate:

- What do these people need to know to be able to interact with us without it being a problem?

- Will they hold this against my family? Will they let their children come over? Should their children be here, given your mate's offense?

- What do you want to say about this disease, your mate's behavior then and now, and the risk your mate is putting others in by being near them.

- If your mate has probation or parole requirements, what do the neighbors or others need to know about that to feel safer around you and your family?

- If the neighbors are being supportive, let them know what they can do to help. Inviting your children to their home for a fun activity or a sleepover can help your children feel some sense of normalcy. Perhaps they can sit with the children while you and your mate have an evening out or go for a walk together.

Sex Offender Registry

When an addict is listed on a sex offender registry, various types of disclosures are required. Most of the public believes that only pedophiles and rapists are listed on the registry. That is not true. A conviction of any sex offense can result in being placed on the registry, often with a legal description of the offense that is unclear about the behavior. For example, "sexual production with a minor" represents dozens of things, one of which might be what your mate did (such as made a video of himself and a seventeen-year-old he thought was twenty-one), but your neighbors don't know that. In some states, judges even require sex offenders to put signs in their yards stating "Danger! A convicted sex offender lives here!" Preparing for being listed and handling people's reactions is important for the addict, partner, children, family, neighbors, and community.

Not every community is ready to support your mate if he has committed a sexual offense, but you may be surprised how people will support him if he is doing everything in his effort to stop his offending behavior and keep himself and his community safe.

If he is on a registry or going to be, it is only a matter of time until someone finds out. First and foremost, your mate and children need to know how to handle the anger and fear of others. Excluding small children, everyone in the family needs to talk about the possibility of violence by uninformed, fearful, and angry people. You mate needs to have his internal voice remind himself that he is not bad (even if he did bad things) and he needs to come from a place of strength, knowing that he has a right to be in his home, his yard. Still, it is important to be wise about what he does. Until he has a group in your community who knows some of his story and is supportive of his efforts to be healthy, it is wise to go places together. Being alone draws suspicion and a single person makes a better target than two or more.

If you and your mate have been friendly with your neighbors in the past and none of them has been a victim of the offense, it is likely they will listen to what the two of you have to say. What has worked best in these cases is to select one or two people or couples who are most likely to listen, learn, and be supportive. Ask those people to meet you and your mate in your home. When they are present tell them that the two of you have something very important you want to tell them and hope they will hear you out before making a judgment. A letter format works well here, too, as people usually will let a person finish the letter before reacting or asking questions and getting distracted by their own confusion or fear. Of course, the addict should read this letter and you should be present. If teenaged children are in the household, they can be present if they want the neighbors to know that they know and the family is working on this together. The recommended contents of the letter are described in detail in the companion book, *Disclosing Secrets: An Addict's Guide for When, to Whom, and How Much to Reveal*. Sometimes it is helpful to have this first conversation with your minister or rabbi or other religious leaders present in your home.

If you and the addict have been very isolated, it is less likely that your neighbors will be supportive. They have no history with him and will be afraid. Each case must be measured within the context of your situation. We do know that people are less likely to re-offend or relapse if they are not isolated. So, your mate needs to find a place where he can share his situation. In most Sex Addicts Anonymous meetings people can talk about these issues. You, too, will benefit from the support of other people. Check into the availability of S-Anon or COSA meetings in your area (See Appendix 2 for contact information for these Twelve-step programs for partners and families of sex addicts).

Here is how the family of one sex offender handled the sex offender registry problem:

When Bill, a junior high school science teacher, was sentenced to twelve years in prison for having a sexual relationship with one of his fourteen-year-old students, his wife Colleen moved in with her parents in a quiet suburban neighborhood. Her parents helped with childcare of her three daughters while Colleen finished college, then graduate school, and became a successful career woman. Colleen's religion did not support divorce or remarriage, so Colleen decided to wait for her husband's release. Every week for twelve years Colleen and the children visited her husband in prison. She also arranged for a counselor to do joint counseling with the couple during additional prison visits.

Because Bill's arrest and conviction were widely reported in the newspapers, Colleen's neighbors were well aware of her circumstances. Over the years they got to know Colleen and her three daughters and came to admire her for her efforts to keep the family together. When it was time for Bill's release, Colleen visited each of the neighbors, beginning with the ones she knew were most supportive, and talked with them about Bill's approaching arrival, about how he had matured in prison and had spent years making amends to his family and regretting his offenses with the young student, and about the plans the family had to make a new life for themselves. She assured them that their children were not at risk, and asked to hear about any concerns they might have. By the time the neighbors were informed by law enforcement that a sex offender was about to live in their neighborhood, they were sufficiently knowledgeable about the situation that it was not a problem either for them or for Bill.

Colleen had for years dreamed about relocating to a new city, one where no-one had heard of Bill or his history, but she realized she would have the most support from the community if she stayed put. Her decision proved to be a good one.

It is not always easy to balance the "rigorous honesty" of addiction recovery and the reality that disclosure in certain circumstances may have adverse consequences that call for careful planning or for nondisclosure. In this chapter we gave you guidelines for getting through this difficult experience. In the next chapter we will describe how to bring together what you have learned so far as you start your new life after disclosure.

Chapter Nine
After Disclosure—What Now?

After disclosure addicts report feeling relief at not having to live the double life, but they are also overwhelmed by the fear of the reactions to the pain they have inflicted. Partners are in shock, hurting beyond belief, and experiencing a wide range of emotions. Some partners are so overwhelmed they become depressed and suicidal, and isolate themselves because of the shame associated with the addict's behavior. Other partners feel threatened and are so angry they cannot tolerate having the addict near them; they often are quick to threaten divorce. The flood of emotions seems overwhelming and couples usually do not know what to do next. A rule of thumb for people early in recovery—*do not make any major decisions in the first year.*

Janis Abrahms Spring, in her book, *After the Affair: Healing the Pain and Rebuilding Trust When a Partner has been Unfaithful*, dramatically describes the hurt partner's initial response as "buried in an avalanche of losses." Partners' subsequent recovery course can vary widely. Partners who came from a relatively healthy background and who are fairly early in their relationship with the addict experience the trauma, but are likely to have a fairly brief recovery course; they don't have to deal with the reawakening of prior trauma and codependency issues, nor with many years of lies and betrayal by the addict. The partner whose trauma of disclosure occurred in a context of prior trauma and resultant codependency features will need to do more extensive work to resolve these pre-existing characteristics and learn more functional ways of coping. If she remains in the relationship it will likely take her longer to regain trust in her mate.

Also, there are likely to be some differences in the recovery work that male and female partners of sex addicts need to do. Men are more likely than women to be able to separate sexual activities from love, while at the same time they may feel more anger and competitiveness (worry) about their own sexual ability and how they measure up sexually against the affair partner (if there was one). When the addict's sexual acting out does not include actual contact with another person they may consider it less of a big deal than do women, who can be just as devastated by an emotional affair as by a physical affair. Men may be in denial about the significance of the affair to their female mate. Men also tend to be less in touch with their feelings and may need more therapy work to overcome this. They might feel a lot of anger, but not recognize the underlying pain and sadness.

An excellent first step for a partner who has discovered or been told about her mate's sex addiction is to get some support for herself. If you do not already have a therapist, find one who is knowledgeable about sex addiction and comfortable with seeing partners. A good resource is the website of the Society for the Advancement of Sexual Health, www.sash.net, which has a list of knowledgeable counselors by state and city. Barbara Steffens and Marsha Means, in their book *Your Sexually Addicted Spouse: How Partners can Cope and Heal*, describe the role that a good therapist will initially provide for you – a professional who will recognize that disclosure or discovery is a traumatic event, validate your pain, acknowledge the trauma you are experiencing from the betrayal of trust, and will support you in dealing with the trauma.

To prevent further deterioration of the relationship, couples need to formulate a plan to keep the relationship on hold. Initially, it is useful to determine if you want a short separation. The idea is to separate so self-repair can be implemented and a support system can be established. The support system needs to both support you *and* hold you accountable as well. In volatile situations, having two places to live for a while is optimal.

Unfortunately, not everyone is in a position to do that. Even in situations in which people can manage their anger, sometimes they need a short time apart. Some homes are large enough so that each member of the couple can have their own private space to go to for self-repair. You may want to stay with friends or family for a few days. Learning to ask for help is a useful skill; this is a time to practice. However you decide to get your space, place a few things there that provide a sense of well-being. Sometimes it is helpful to print statements that represent how you want to think and respond—positive self-talk. This will help in times when you cannot easily remember how you want to respond to situations.

Boundaries and Agreements

To reduce further damage to the relationship, it is important to agree when you will talk with each other and how you will manage yourself during times when you are talking. If you feel that face-to-face discussions are too painful early on, then write notes to each other. If living separately, designate certain times to talk by phone or, if computer use is not an issue, correspond by email or texting. Because this is a cooling-off period, it is appropriate to decide what subject matter is off limits for now. For example, you may want to postpone intense discussions about the disclosure information you received until both of you have a support system in place and have had time to reflect about the impact the addiction and trauma have had on your relationships, and most of all, on you.

It is important to talk about the acting-out behaviors, but we recommend you do that in therapy sessions. If that is not possible, delay the conversations until you've had some time to heal and get clear about your feelings and your hopes for the future.

When speaking about day-to-day issues, be careful not to fall into the trap of what John Gottman, Ph.D., who has studied married couples for years, calls the "Four Deadly Horsemen." Too often when couples are hostile with each other, they revert to four destructive styles of interacting. These do not always show up in this order, but generally the conversation starts in a harsh way. One party *criticizes* the other harshly rather than presenting a complaint. A complaint describes a specific behavior whereas a criticism contains harsh or negative words about your partner's personality, and frequently adds on some criticism from a previous situation unrelated to the specific behavior in question.

For example, a complaint might be:

> *Len, I am frustrated because you agreed to pick up the kids from school and bring them home by 6:00 P.M., but you are consistently late.*

In contrast, a criticism would sound like this:

I cannot believe that you can't get this one thing right. What the hell is wrong with you? This is so simple; if you really cared you would get the kids back to me as we agreed. This is just like all the other times you've screwed up—no wonder I can't trust you.

Another negative style is to use *contempt* when you complain or criticize. Sarcasm and cynicism are passive-aggressive ways to show contempt. They include mocking your partner, using hostile or inappropriate humor, being belligerent, rolling your eyes, and name calling—all of which send the signal that you are disgusted by your partner. Using contempt inevitably leads to more conflict or another "horseman"—stonewalling.

Stonewalling is when the listener gives the talker all the cues that he or she is not listening. There is no eye contact, no head nods, and no verbal encouragement—such as saying "uh-huh" or asking questions for clarification. The listener sits like a stone wall and looks down or away the whole time the other person is talking or goes to their room and shuts the door without explanation.

The fourth horseman is *defensiveness*. Defending one's actions is a normal response when a person is attacked, but in cases in which someone continues to criticize, defending oneself usually makes matters worse. Certainly addict is the designated "bad guy" and needs to be accountable for his hurtful behaviors. However, both you and the addict have been in a dance of self-destructive behaviors and eventually you *both* have to learn to identify and change those behaviors, but for now, you have to accommodate more.

If you catch yourself using any of these styles, call a timeout and tell your mate you need a break for self-repair because you don't like the way you are thinking or behaving. One way to engage in self-repair is to learn to stay grounded internally.

Personal Healing: Self-Repair through Internal Grounding

We want you to think about your authentic self. This is the person you strive to be—the healthy person in recovery. Your authentic self operates from a set of values that guide your behaviors. Below are some examples of values that would guide your behavior as an authentic person.

- A goal of all healthy people is to maintain a clear sense of their authentic selves. This is especially true when the heat gets turned up in a fight or when your brain gets hijacked by old memories. As you work though issues, you and your partner will become more and more important to each other. That makes the threat of losing your mate even more frightening. So when you call a time out for self-repair, remind yourself who you strive to be as an authentic person. Review your new values and tell yourself you refuse to return to presenting an inaccurate picture of yourself.

- Think about your anxieties, limitations, and shortcomings by identifying what is making you anxious or fearful. Determine what you can and cannot do. (Remember the Serenity Prayer— "God, grant me the serenity to accept the things I cannot change, courage to change the things I can, and wisdom to know the difference" –this is a good time to say it!) This will prevent your anxiety from driving your decisions or immobilizing you. I like to say another little prayer when I am stuck. "Help!" or the longer version is "Higher Power, I don't know exactly how to fix this. Please show me the way. If I can't fix it or if it isn't my job to fix it, help me to get through this with integrity and doing no harm."

- Hold yourself accountable. Identify what you are doing that is not helping the situation. Are you afraid? If so, are they reasonable fears about what is going on, or are they connected to something from your family of origin? Are you being selfish, trying to manipulate the situation, engaging in behaviors that you know will make things worse? What other options do you have that will make things better? What would you be doing if you really wanted to show your mate that you love him or her?

- Acknowledge your projections and thinking errors. Admit when you are wrong—don't wait for your mate to do so first, or ever, for that matter.

- Tolerate the discomfort. It is the way to grow. Support yourself through positive affirmations. Pray for your mate. Soothe yourself through meditation, humming, or singing; have a special coloring book and color yourself to safety.

If this doesn't work at first, you just need some practice. Eventually you will find it will work for you. In the meantime, to create a safer playing field for discussions, the following guidelines may help:

- Be ready to call "time out for self-repair" if discussions become attack and defend games. Practice self-repair through the steps outlined above. Be sure to agree upon a time to continue talking later.
- To talk about painful issues, have an adult third person present if you are not able to have these discussions without becoming angry.
- When discussing, stick to the issues at hand until you get resolution or agree that you are stuck and need to cool off or get help before moving to another topic.
- Don't blame each other. Talk about feelings first. You may want to use the behavioral change request form outlined below in these discussions.
- If you cannot talk without getting out of control, agree to limit your contact to letters, emails, or texts.
- Set specific hours you can be reached by phone.

If your separation is for more than a few days, establish ground rules for dealing with day-to-day responsibilities. Who will pay which bills? How will the needs of your children be met? If one parent is the primary care taker, how will respite and visitation be managed? What are the arrangements for visiting with the pets? Who will take the car to the tire repair shop? Initially, how long is the separation?

To determine who should do what, make a list of all the things you were responsible for in day-to-day maintenance in your household. If logistics allow, it may be easier to keep doing what you have done. Otherwise, decide who is best at what. Additionally, if this is an area where the addict can "stretch" to show his commitment by handling new responsibilities, he might volunteer to take those on. Or if your spouse has been an over-functioning partner, you might invite him to give up some of his responsibilities so you can demonstrate that you are totally committed to being more responsible.

If you have children, agree to treat each other like friends in front of them, no matter how angry or disappointed you are with yourself or your mate. You already know that it's not good for your children to be put in the middle of your pain, and have probably reproached yourself more than once for doing just that. If you can follow this suggestion, you will feel much better about yourself.

Regarding your sexual and emotional connection with your mate, you might have a list of "off-limits" items. This might include not being touched or kissed. Some partners don't want to be told that the addict loves them—others want to hear it and see behaviors that demonstrate this. Obviously, these items are an individual preference. If you have an "off-limits" list, your mate needs to abide by by it even if it may seem overly punitive to him. He needs to recognize that, during the first few weeks or months after disclosure, partners are frequently still in shock. It takes a while to even understand how they feel.

Because you have been lied to so much, it is critical that you get validation that your feelings are normal for this stage of the healing. This can happen in therapy, in Twelve-Step groups or other support groups, with a minister or rabbi, or perhaps with a best friend. You will want to know why the addict did what he did—but rarely is any explanation enough to take the pain away. For now accept that he did not do what he did because of you. He did it because he could not handle his emotions in a healthier way. Now he has a chance to learn how to do just that. He will also learn that his experiences in his family of origin most likely contributed to his inability to manage emotional distress effectively. These lessons help take away his shame and self-blame.

During the first year, when you complain or get caught in your post-traumatic stress by remembering events of the past, it is especially helpful for your mate to acknowledge that what he did was wrong, to reassure you that you have every right to feel the way you do, and to ask you what he can do today to make things better. It is also important for you and your mate to share what you are each learning about yourself through recovery, so find a time to do that.

Managing Emotional States

As you can see, the process of disclosure is an opportunity for both partners to "grow yourself up" or mature in ways that help you personally and help your relationship. It is your responsibility for your own healing. In times of crisis, we often mismanage our emotions and make matters worse. Someone who is able to manage emotional states is said to have high emotional intelligence. According to Daniel Goleman (2011), that means the person can:

- Recognize a feeling as it happens.

- Manage emotions by soothing yourself and bounce back quickly from life's challenges and minor crises.

- Motivate self to have self-control in order to delay gratification and control impulses.

- Recognize emotions in others and have empathy for them.

- Manage your own emotional state when the other person can't manage his or her own emotions.

Emotions that are most often mismanaged are anger, fear, shame, and power. The emotional state that encourages mismanaged anger the most is shame. Shame is guilt's big brother. Guilt is feeling awful for having gone too far or for not having done enough. Shame is feeling inadequate for not being worthy enough. Underlying shame are confusion and a feeling of abandonment. Shame makes us want to either blame someone so we don't have to look at our part in the situation or get revenge for how someone hurt us. But getting revenge doesn't mean getting over what has happened. Also, getting revenge never feels very good for long. Instead, it builds a wall around us that doesn't allow healing love to penetrate.

Anger can be helpful to give us energy, but after a while it gets in the way of healing. Because of the intensity of the feeling, we are seduced into believing that the anger is making us stronger when it actually can diminish our personal power. When we mismanage anger we get caught up in the obsession of the events surrounding the betrayal and we relive the pain of the disclosure over and over. If this goes unchecked we continue to feel powerless. And that is a move right back to addictive and co-addictive behavior.

Partners, if you are having problems with obsessing about what the addict has done or about your own behaviors or reactions, you may want to implement an activity to help yourself reduce those invasive

AFTER DISCLOSURE—WHAT NOW?

thoughts. An exercise used by many therapists allows your creative side to come out. Susan Forward (1999) describes a version of this and calls the exercise "The Movie in Your Mind."

First, make an imaginary movie using the obsessive, intrusive thoughts and pictures that tromp endlessly through your head. You can use the images you have in your head of your addict acting out in some manner. Make the movie as vivid as other visions you experience in your head most of the time.

Next, become a movie critic. Write a synopsis of the movie as if you were writing it for *The Today Show* or some magazine. Then write a review of the movie. Totally trash the movie, being critical of the "actors," the location, and the story line. Make it really scathing, using humor as much as possible. This will start the process of reducing the power of these thoughts in your head.

Next, empower yourself with your remote control. Yes, actually use the remote control you have at home. Carry the remote with you at all times as a symbol of having control over your thoughts (and of the thoughts of the addict that live in your head). When the thoughts invade your mind, push the off button, just as you would if you were turning off the television. Next, see the image fade to black or automatically turn the screen to black. I find it helpful to see the image, then close your eyes and see the black of your closed eyelids—focusing intently on the black screen. Continue to see the black for 30 seconds—in that 30 seconds you are in control.

If you have numerous scenes invading your head, allow yourself to watch your addict partner, tolerating the pain for a few minutes, then turn it off, see the black screen and say to yourself, "I am getting better, I am gaining control over my thoughts and my life. I will heal. No matter what, I will heal." And you will!

Decrease the time you watch the movie and increase the time the screen is black each day. As the "director" of this movie, you can do what you want with the movie. You may have a positive memory of you being with your mate sometime in the past (not a romantic memory), one in which you felt authentic. You can practice changing the channel with your remote from the obsessive acting out movie to a new movie of you being authentic. Start to see something that makes you feel good about yourself. That something may be a beautiful place you've been to with or without your mate. See yourself there, feel what you need to feel, hear what you need to hear, say what you need to say to feel empowered. That's the movie you want to watch. The more you consciously choose to replace the acting out movie with one that empowers you, the sooner you will be able to have your life back. Before long, you'll find that you can go to black or change the scene whenever you want to.

When we mismanage any emotion, it is often related not only to the current situation but some past event as well. For example, most people have experienced some type of childhood trauma. Birth, after all, is traumatic. But even in the best of families, natural events occur: pets die, teachers or coaches can be harsh, in some families children are expected to do far more than is reasonable. Others are sexually or physically abused. Unless a caring adult is around to help a young person make sense of what has happened, the child will make up stories in his or her mind about why and how something happened—usually taking the blame for things going bad. This self-blame then becomes the way the person sees traumatic events that happen in the present. In other words, the events of today are experienced with the eyes and emotions of the child who was traumatized earlier in life. The person stays stuck in the past and mismanages the emotional state of the present.

Learn from the Past, Stay in the Present

One way to "grow yourself up" is to learn from the past and stay in the present. Anytime you feel that past emotions may be interfering with taking appropriate action in the present, below are some steps you can take:

1. What am I feeling right now?
2. What does this remind me of?
3. What feelings are underneath what I am experiencing now? (Under anger we often find fear and sadness.)
4. How can I best express my feelings to maximize healing and grow?

AFTER DISCLOSURE—WHAT NOW?

5. Do I need to hold someone accountable or am I over-reacting because this reminds me of the past? (If it is reminding me of the past, is there someone from my past I need to hold accountable?)
6. What is my part in helping to create the situation?
7. What can I learn from the situation?
8. How am I powerful in the situation?
9. How do I want to transition to another place in the relationship with myself and my partner?

Once you are able to really figure out what is happening in a given situation, you can then take appropriate action. Instead of mismanaging an emotional state to put distance between you, hold yourself and the other person accountable. Remember also that you are most powerful when you can come from love instead of anger or fear.

How To Hold Someone Else Accountable

1. Write a detailed description of the event or situation about which you experience pain, anger, or another powerful feeling.
2. What meaning did you give to the event? How did you interpret the other person's behavior? (This is a great exercise to teach to kids as well.)
3. How did you make matters worse for yourself?
4. What do you want the other person to do today to help you to heal?

Re-read this again and determine if you are calm enough to discuss this with the other person. If so, ask for an appointment to share this important information. Otherwise return to self-soothing activities until you are managing your emotional discomfort.

If your mate or another person has asked you to be accountable and you feel defensive in response, then you will want to follow the steps listed below. Remember, being defensive doesn't work.

Holding Myself Accountable

1. Repeat what you heard about what you did that your mate or someone is asking you to be accountable for.

2. Acknowledge that what you did had an impact on the other person. Look for ways in which this person has a good point and agree with anything you can. (You can always agree that he (or she) seems upset and after hearing his description and the meaning to him you can tell him you understand how he would feel that way.)

3. Humbly state you are sorry and ask for forgiveness.

4. If this person has requested something of you, tell him if you can fulfill her request. If not, suggest a few other options you can do.

Sometimes we use the "behavioral change request" activity in the same way. It is a common communication exercise that many therapists recommend, but has a built-in accountability clause for you as well.

Behavior Change Request

Use this exercise any time you need to talk to your mate about a sensitive issue. It holds both of you accountable for your parts in the situation. Until it becomes easy, write the answers to each line, and then ask your mate for time to process.

1. I feel frustrated when you _____

2. Other emotions I feel are _____

3. I make matters worse by _____

4. To hide my fear that _____

5. I also feel sad about _____

6. What I really want from you today to make this better is _____

7. What I expect of myself in this situation is _____.

Distrust and suspiciousness are to be expected in the early stages after disclosure. Although some therapists may recommend doing some detective work to diminish the fears of the partner, we find this type of behavior often consumes the energy of the partner and produces a probation officer/offender relationship for the couple. This keeps the addict and partner on unequal footing, which is often a trigger for both parties to resume old behaviors.

Sometimes the partner can't get unstuck from obsessing about the addict's past behaviors and projects them on everything that happens in the present. Often an addict will offer to take a polygraph test in her presence, if that will help. Sometimes just offering to do this "objective" measure is enough insurance or proof to the partner that she can move on with her work. Our research has shown that when the addicted person undergoes a polygraph test as part of his/her relapse prevention and as a way to reassure his/her partner, the polygraph results are seen as helpful to both the partner and addict.

Similarly, the drug addict may be asked to submit to a urine drug screen, which is a test for various drugs of abuse in a urine specimen. This test is routinely used in physician monitoring programs and in other recovery situations. A series of negative results (i.e., no illicit substances are found in the urine) establishes a track record of recovery; some addicts find it useful to have this outside monitoring until they learn to manage their emotions rather than act out.

Rebuilding Trust

One of the most devastating consequences of disclosure of secrets is the loss of trust experienced by the partner. Of course, it is a mistake to consider the cause of the loss of trust to be the disclosure—that is only the precipitating factor; it is analogous to blaming the messenger for the bad news. The underlying causes of the loss of trust are the addict's behavior and the lies that were used to cover it up. Words and promises will not do it—changed behaviors and evidence of honesty are the keys to rebuilding trust.

In order for you to begin to trust again, you have to believe that the addict intends to change. More importantly, you need to believe that your mate has the competency to implement the changes. You might believe he wants to change but you may not think he can do it. You won't trust him again until you are convinced he has the skill to do what he says he intends to do.

A commonly heard complaint by addicts is, "I've been toeing the line for six weeks, yet my partner says she can't trust me as far as she can throw me. I'm no longer engaging in my addictive behavior, I come home early every day or phone my wife if I'm delayed, I participate in therapy and self-help groups. What more do I have to do?" The answer is, more of the same, for another year or two. It doesn't seem fair, but your mate needs to think about how long he has been acting out. For most addicts, comparatively, a couple of years is not much. Rebuilding trust after disclosure of a serious transgression is a process, one that takes an average of two years according to research on recovering couples. (Schneider & Schneider, 1999.). At six weeks, the process is only beginning.

Here are some criteria by which trust is evaluated. These are things your mate can do to restore your trust. It's a good idea to sit down and discuss these criteria with your mate so that he understands your expectations and so you know what he is willing to do:

1. **Be Honest.** This means practicing no deception, no longer leading a secret life apart from you, and no longer telling lies or omitting the truth when talking with others about events. Addicts become so accustomed to lying that it becomes second nature. They frequently lie, even about matters where there is no reason to lie and no cost to telling the truth. After years of watching him lie, dissemble, stretch and bend the truth, and cover up various actions, it's not surprising you don't trust him. He has to build a new track record to combat the miserable one that you had much experience observing. One of the most effective trust-rebuilding strategies for the addict is to adopt a lifestyle of rigorous honesty. For example, if you asked him to pick up a carton of milk on the way home and he forgot, his previous approach upon arrival home might have been to tell you, "I got held up at the office and didn't have time," or some other such excuse. Instead, try telling the truth: "I'm so sorry, it just slipped my mind." If the two of you are shopping at the hardware store and the clerk gives your mate an extra dollar bill in change, he needs to give it back. When you observe him being honest in the small ways day after day, week after week, you will be more likely to believe that he will be honest in the big ways.

2. **Be Transparent**. This means your mate's life is an open book to you and that you both have the same goals regarding your life together and for healing as a couple. Your mate should seek to understand you, to know you better so that he can respond to your needs when asked. When you request information from him, he is totally forthcoming.

3. **Be Accountable**. He does what he says or promises and he has proof of what he says. That means any activity he has with another person can be verified. He is no longer vague or unreachable. It may even mean that he gives his accountability buddy permission to speak to you about matters of concern to you. Tell your mate when he (or she) is providing too much information in his attempts to be accountable, especially in the first year. Over time, as trust builds, you both will get into a rhythm –but he will need to continue actively working his recovery and remain accountable. Otherwise, he will be at risk of slips, and slips will lead to relapse.

4. **Be Ethical**. The addict needs to make his standards high for himself, to have integrity in all he does and to be fair.

5. **Build An Alliance**. We know that family, specifically partners play an important role in helping get addicts to take steps towards recovery. After a betrayal, it is difficult for partners to believe that the addict will ever be trustworthy enough to trust again but partners want their mate to "have their backs". Your mate wants you on his or her side – and you want him on your side. That is what trust is about. Having you on his side means that you have evidence that he no longer operates out of self-interest and does not form coalitions against you. It means that you believe he has your best interest at heart.

These criteria are based on the work of John Gottman (2012) in his book *The Science of Trust*. He also points out that for couples to really heal they must work toward more equality within the relationship. Early on this is difficult. The more you can replace conflict avoidance with constructive conflict management, the greater your chances of feeling more equal in the relationship.

While you have heard repeatedly in this book that you and your mate need to work on your individual recovery, we need to remind you that for your relationship to be satisfying and long lasting, your commitment should include working towards interdependence. Counting on each other to get your central needs met, building new goals together, and utilizing more positive self-talk about the relationship help to strengthen the relationship. It is important to cherish your mate, instead of trashing him or her; to be grateful for this journey rather than resentful for the amount of work and pain that has to be endured. This is a gradual process.

Ending the Relationship

No matter how hard you try, in some cases, the relationship doesn't get better, and neither the partner nor the addict seems to get better. The couple falls back into old patterns of relating, partners remain critical and addicts remain defensive. It seems easier to keep up the fight or just submit and withdraw. There is no a mutuality of needs, emotional need is not processed, and the hurt doesn't heal. Rather than turning towards each other to try to solve problems, there is turning away and no restoration of trust. In these cases, to get better the addict and partner have to end their destructiveness by ending the relationship. Sometimes this is clear early on; other times it takes years.

If it does happen, then it is important to grieve the loss. Perhaps it is the loss of the fantasy that one day you would have a happy, satisfying relationship. Perhaps it is the loss of your children for long periods of time. It can be loss over many things, but it is still important to understand the impact the loss has on you. Seek help to talk about the pain and anger (and other emotions that will be generated by the loss). Start new rituals for holidays and vacations with recovering friends. Realize that you can still treat your mate in friendly ways and above all, have integrity about what you do. That is part of your recovery.

Recommitment

After a lot of hard work and self-searching, most couples want to reconcile and recommit to their relationship. This is after caring has been re-established through relationship-enhancing behaviors. Research tells us that the prognosis is good for couples in which both are committed to making the journey of recovery together (Gordon & Baucom, 2003). True intimacy starts after you learn how to trust yourself and manage your emotions in healthy ways rather than fall back into old ways of thinking and acting.

Couples who survive the first two years or so of recovery are surprised at how strong they have become as individuals. They are ready to recommit to having a marriage that is realistic and a healthy place to grow as individuals. Research indicates that couples who stay together and report long-term happiness have goals for their relationship in addition to goals for individual growth. They have established caring, commitment, and a process of compassionate communication. We know how terrible your emotional pain has been. Our hope is that now you are on the way to true friendship with your mate.

Stay Positive

It is difficult to stay positive when so much pain and shame occurs. As part of your daily inventory, make sure you identify something that you are grateful for right now. Also remember your strengths and achievements, not just your challenges. Remember what the faces look like of five people who love you, warts and all.

Hang around with positive people. In his uplifting book *The 4:8 Principle: The Secret to A Joy-Filled Life*, Tommy Newberry shares a visual example he uses with teens about choosing friends wisely. While on stage he gets a volunteer to let Tommy try to pick him up onto the stage using just one arm. After some exaggerated attempts with no success, he then invites the young person to try to pull him down from the stage just using one finger – an easier task. The audience quickly gets the message – it is far easier to be pulled down than lifted up. This is especially true early in recovery. What we have also learned from research with recovering people is that when people who have good recovery hang out together, they tend to stay sober longer, and to be happier.

So be alert to who is lifting you up and who is pulling you down. Look for people whose integrity is high, who share you values about recovery and demonstrate joyful living. Look for those who will also bring the best out in you and will challenge you to honor your recovery principles. And finally, rather than only being grateful about getting something that is missing, try appreciating what you are presented with. Life is as easy as we make it.

References

Bader, E, and Pearson, P, *In Quest of The Mythical Mate*. New York: Brunner Mazel.1988.

Forward, Susan. *When Your Lover is a Liar: Healing the Wounds of Deception and Betrayal.* 1999.

Glass, Shirley. 2001, personal communication

Goleman, D. *Emotional Intelligence*. New York: Bantam Books, 1995.

Gottman, J. *Why Marriages Succeed or Fail.* New York: Simon & Schuster, 1994.

Gottman, John, *The Science of Trust* New York: W.W. Norton,2012

Gordon, K. C. & Baucom, D. H. (2003). Forgiveness and marriage. *American Journal of Family Therapy, 31*, 179-199.

Newberry, Tommy. *The 4:8 Principle: The Secret to a Joy-filled Life.* Carol Stream, IL:Tyndale House Publisher, Inc., 2007.

Schneider, J. and Schneider, B.H. *Sex, Lies, and Forgiveness: Couples Speak on Healing from Sex Addiction*, Third Edition, Tucson, Ariz.: Recovery Resources Press, 2005.

SIECUS Report, Washington DC: Sex Information and Education Council of the United States,1995.

Spring, Janis Abrahms. *After the Affair: Healing the Pain and Rebuilding Trust When a Partner has been Unfaithful.* New York, Harper Collins, 1996.

Steffens, Barbara and Marsha Means. *Your Sexually Addicted Spouse: How Partners Can Cope and Heal.* Far Hills, NJ: New Horizons Press, 2009.

Chapter Ten
For Helping Professionals

Because disclosure of sexual information tends to be the most difficult for professionals to handle, this chapter refers to working with sexual infidelity. The information provided is appropriate to most addictive behavior.

Relationship distress in couples in which a disclosure or discovery of extramarital behavior has occurred frequently motivates one or both members of the couple to seek professional help. Because this type of disclosure is taken so personally by the partner, we have added this chapter for professionals helping couples deal with revelations of a sexual nature. The guidelines outlined in this chapter are appropriate for other types of disclosures as well.

There are many similarities between non-addicted and addicted couples seeking help to work through the labyrinth of emotions and decisions. However, there are several special needs of the addict. The therapist's actions can be instrumental in helping both the individual and the couple make progress towards healing.

Differences Between Addicted and Non-addicted Couples

Almost all unfaithful mates struggle with disclosure. As with addicts, they do not want to hurt their partners nor get into trouble, so their tendency is to avoid opening up. Yet, most of the books on surviving infidelity promote honesty about the behavior (mostly affairs). This makes sense because the majority of these books are authored by women who have survived an affair. Most men or women who have had an affair would prefer that they did not have to disclose. Unfortunately, guilt or evidence often prompts telling. In addition to the unfaithful mate's guilt, there exists a wide range of emotions for both people in the relationship.

We have little information about the number of people who get involved in affairs, or go on sexual binges of some type outside the primary relationship and if not caught, do not tell. In the past, several prominent public figures were caught being unfaithful and made matters worse by denying their involvement with an affair partner or their extensive cybersex or pornography use. In the more recent past, many of these high-profile cases have started with early admission in hopes of cooling down the media frenzy. While that seems like progress, anyone paying attention to the partner of these (mostly) men, some of whom stand dutifully at their husband's side as he publicly divulges his transgression, can see from their body language that they are in distress.

Why, then, do we promote disclosure for addicts and their partners? Partly because of the outcome of our research: Most addicts and partners agree that telling was useful and in most cases helped them stay sober, gave them enough hope to stay involved in each other's lives in healthy ways, and demonstrated the motivation to change.

Another very important reason is because addictive behaviors are repetitive in nature. Being addicted means that your brain is formatted to seek out situations in which the brain chemistry will be altered enough to ensure an altered mood. The majority of addicts cannot manage to gain any health if they are still sexually involved outside the relationship—they experience too much shame and guilt, which are strong stimuli for relapse. Just as an alcoholic cannot hang out in a bar and expect to abstain from alcohol, sex addicts cannot hang out where their "drug" of choice is, without risking acting out again. Most addicts and partners find that honesty helps them remain connected to their recovery efforts. Disclosure seems to offer hope—and almost a form of insurance for the addict and his or her partner. To lie or continue to lie just fuels the engine that runs the addiction and further traumatizes the partner.

Therefore, we do encourage addicts to come clean to their mates (and vice-versa) in almost all cases. On the other hand, if someone is not an addict, we examine the context and meaning of the infidelity before making any recommendation about disclosure. If a client requests guidance about whether to reveal an affair, some questions worthy of discussion in individual therapy session are:

- Is the affair over?

- Does the client still have any contact with the affair partner, or does his or her spouse?

- Does the client still have strong emotions about the affair partner?

- How did the affair impact the couple's relationship?

- What lies were used to cover up the affair?

- Did the partner suspect, and if so, how much energy and additional lying was necessary to disarm the partner's suspicions? (For example, was the partner accused of imagining things, paranoia, etc. that perhaps contributed to the partner's loss of self-esteem?)

- Is this the only affair the client has had, or has this been a recurring pattern?

- Does the past affair have any impact on the couple's current relationship?

- How comfortable does the client feel about continuing to conceal the affair?

- What is the meaning for the client of continuing not to disclose, and of disclosing?

- What does the client believe will be the positive as well as negative consequences of revealing the affair (on himself, on the spouse, on the relationship)?

- What does the client believe will be the positive and negative consequences of continuing *not* to divulge the affair (on himself, on the spouse, on the relationship)?

By clarifying the reasons for the client's consideration of disclosure, you can help him or her decide if it would be the right thing to do. By asking about other affairs, you may be able to identify an addiction problem, in which case telling is recommended, and may itself constitute an intervention that will lead to addiction treatment for the unfaithful spouse.

If your client is someone in a committed relationship or marriage who suspects her or his mate of infidelity, you need to consider in your differential diagnosis the possibility that her (or his) mate is a sex addict who has repeatedly lied to her. If she complains that her mate's interest in sex with her has diminished, consider that he may be getting his sexual needs met in other ways. If you are seeing both partners, keep in mind that the possibility that one is keeping secrets from the other, and make it clear to each client in advance what you will do if one of them reveals to you secrets that he or she is keeping from the other. We will discuss these issues below.

Before even embarking on this discussion, however, we recommend that you ask yourself the following questions:

- Have you (the therapist) had an extramarital affair yourself, or have you been the betrayed partner?
- How does your personal experience about affairs, secrets, and lies affect your feelings and beliefs about the appropriateness of the client's disclosing the affair?

Understanding your own feelings about disclosure will allow you to counsel the client more objectively and more effectively.

The Role of the Therapist

As a therapist, it is not your role to side with either the partner or the addict. It is tempting to side with the partner because the addict has done the betraying. However, this puts the therapist in a triangulated position and allows the couple to focus on blaming or proving their point through the therapist rather than dealing with their own issues within the context of the relationship. Early in therapy, the couple looks to the therapist as the all-knowing expert. Sharing information about what you have learned through the literature, research, and your own clinical experience with couples dealing with addiction can be useful in order to give the couple hope and help them be realistic about what to expect.

The therapist helps to interpret what is happening and discusses the differences between how men and women view and interpret situations. She or he validates each one's reality and the intensity of their feelings. As a coach, the therapist offers strategies to help the couple communicate more effectively (especially the listening and reflecting part of communicating). Incorporating cognitive behavioral exercises will help correct thinking errors and develop skills to build emotional competence. Personal responsibility can be enhanced by teaching the couple skills for holding self and each other accountable.

As the couple progresses you will see them able to move from the attack-defend mode of interacting to productively handling disagreements or difficult issues. Gradually, they will address problems without blaming or bringing up past betrayals. Having moved from interventionist in the early crisis phase, to educator and then coach during the rebuilding stage, the therapist's role near the end of therapy changes to cheerleader, letting the couple practice what they have learned.

How Long in Therapy

Working with these couples is a long-term commitment on everyone's part. It takes between two and five years for recovery to really get integrated into the lives of the couple. Couples therapy helps the relationship grow and sustain the stormy times. We have found that couples most often enter therapy for at least twelve weeks, make progress, and then come back bi-monthly, then monthly for the first year. We typically see couples for monthly maintenance or as crises arise. Couples can benefit from support groups through their local church or synagogue or Recovering Couples Anonymous (see Appendix 2).

Crisis Intervention and Early Therapy

Your introduction to a couple often begins with a telephone call from the partner, who reports a crisis—his infidelity. Ask her when and how she found out, and if there has been an ongoing problem regarding sex in the marriage. If the addict calls, it is usually because the partner has discovered something about his sexual activities, and a major disruption of the marriage has resulted. Ask if the addict thinks he has a serious problem, if he has sought help for the problem and if so, is he still in therapy. Determine if he is still acting out. If yes, then schedule an individual session to assess his commitment to getting into recovery.

The partner is usually in a state of shock, either full of rage and anger or devastated and hopeless. She may vacillate between these emotional states, become anxious, and phone you day and night, weekends and holidays. While listening to her is vital to the process, your ability to model some healthy boundary-setting is equally as important. Assure her that some feelings of desperation and chaos are normal for this period and help her develop a plan for coping with them, including postponing calling you until a designated time. Help her identify a support system by recommending S-Anon, COSA, or Al-Anon meetings (see Appendix 2 for support groups) and clarifying with her who may be safe to share this information with.

In the first few sessions (or in those frantic phone calls) it is helpful to reduce her fear by validating her experience and reassuring her that she is not crazy and that self-care is of the utmost importance. Help her establish obtainable goals in these areas.

In our study, most respondents did see a therapist. In fact, most saw more than one. The partners reported that the most important and useful part of seeing a therapist was being supported and feeling heard. Specifically, several partners commented that helpful therapists established a safe atmosphere in which they felt free to ask questions at any time and in which their suspicions were validated. Partners indicated that the therapists allowed them to make choices.

The second valuable type of advice was to take care of themselves and to recognize that the addict's behavior was not the partner's fault. Partners told us it was helpful for them to be told to give yourself time and space to heal, not to make rash decisions, how to set boundaries, and that self-worth comes from inside, not from other people.

In contrast, addicts reported that the most useful advice was what and how to tell. Some (60%) thought that advice to be honest and tell everything was the most useful. Rather than demand that the addict disclose, a persistent, gentle coaching to share information with the partner was seen as the most motivating. The therapist discouraged keeping secrets, warning that secrets are destructive and severely damage trust. Therapists also helped addicts make better choices by considering many options. Most often though, respondents reported the most useful advice was that honesty is the best way to rebuild the relationship

Help the addict identify his values and formulate ideas about how honesty can be helpful to him in his relationship with his partner and his recovery. Have him be specific about setting goals for honesty.

Although most people in our study reported their experience with advice from therapists to be satisfactory, those who responded to the question about least helpful advice spoke of the impact and seriousness of disclosure for both the addict and the partner. The primary negative theme identified for both addict and partner was lack of knowledge and skill by the therapist. This included lack of responsiveness to the emotional condition of the partner. Below are some comments by partners that illustrate the seriousness of the situation for the partner:

> *Another therapist counseled my husband and me, but she didn't know that it was an addiction. Instead, she encouraged me to be a better sexual partner and support his habits.*
>
> *When I found out my husband prefers men or children, I was really devastated. My self-esteem was shaky and that finished it off. I was afraid for my children. I didn't think my husband would stay in our home. Months later my psychiatrist told me he was a pedophile—by then I was so depressed I was planning to kill myself and my children.*
>
> *I was so angry, but isolated. I needed to talk about my feelings, but his behavior was all we could see. Maybe disclosure should follow preparation. This was such a dangerous time for me.*
>
> *The first two therapists did not address my need to ask more. I saw a psychologist for a period of time. He was ill-prepared to help me. He questioned my aversion to knowing the details. It confused me.*
>
> *I felt I let my children down enormously by dragging them through all the sordid details. Early, I should have been cautioned about who I disclosed to and advised to connect up with S-Anon groups. I acted inappropriately by making several phone calls to two women he'd been with.*

Obviously from these comments, the serious nature of the emotional state of the partners was not enough of a concern for the therapist. Assess the emotional state of the partner before moving forward with further disclosure or before letting the partner leave after a difficult session. Establish a firm goal with her about safety and check for suicidal ideation.

To further assess the case, it can be helpful to give each client a take-home questionnaire at the end of the first session. Questionnaires can be helpful not only to gain information, especially with sexual addiction cases, but as a means of letting each partner "vent." Ask about the type and level of current disruption, abuse during childhood, sexual history including other outside sexual and emotional involvement prior to marriage, sexual behavior and satisfaction within the marriage, other marital satisfaction issues, and how the couple attempts to enhance the relationship. Maintain strict confidentiality about information in the forms. If you determine that some information contained in the questionnaire needs to be shared with the spouse, work with the individual to come to that decision. It is much more useful for the client to realize that himself or herself than for you to demand it. If the homework is not completed, it may be a sign of no privacy at home or a lack of commitment to the process by one or both parties.

After trust has been broken, couples often struggle with what to do about the marriage. It is common to see the partner beset with fear that she will be hurt again or will not be able to heal from the betrayal. She is likely to threaten to leave, want him out of the house, leave herself, or become so hypervigilant that she becomes obsessed by his every move. Reassure couples that their ambivalence and fear about the future of the relationship is normal at this stage. Establish an agreement to not do anything about leaving for three to six months. We recommend waiting a year, but most couples have a difficult time postponing this decision for what seems like such a lengthy time. Couples in early recovery are usually more comfortable agreeing to sit tight for three to six months, and then reassess where they are. At that time, they can recommit to continuing to work on their marriage and perhaps increase their level of commitment to each other. You should also recognize, and advise the couple, that the real recovery takes between two and five years.

Our research and experience indicate that rarely does an addict reveal all during the initial disclosure. He is either afraid of the outcome so only tells what he thinks is enough to get by, or he doesn't remember all his acting out and the lies he told to cover up his actions.

Reiterate to the couple that more than one disclosure is probable and set up a system by which past events can be discussed. To deal with the likelihood that the addict will eventually remember more material or may gradually come to recognize the need to ackowleldge additional matters, agree on a schedule of perhaps once per month for the first three to six months for further revelation of past events and discussion of how the addiction has impacted both their lives.

Addiction is a chronic, relapsing condition; it takes time for the addict to learn to manage it. The partner needs to understand this, and to create a plan proactively for self-care, should a setback take place. If the addict has a slip or relapse, new disclosures should be done as soon as possible. Keeping the information secret will only make the partner trust the addict less. In our most recent research on disclosure of relapse, in couples where the addict admitted the relapse before the partner discovered it, both reported greater satisfaction in the relationship and higher levels of trust.

Recognize that despite preparation, any further disclosure is a setback for the partner. Nonetheless, if she can avoid punishing the addict for being honest, this will increase his level of emotional confidence and be empowering for her. If he continues to relapse, she may have to re-evaluate her desire to stay in a marriage in which the person will not use the tools he has been taught to keep himself healthy.

Early on, suggest that the addict clear the home of as many triggers and paraphernalia as possible. Careful attention to this can be a powerful statement to the partner that the addict is serious about changing. For example, if online sexual activities were part of his repertoire before recovery, the addict can move the computer to a public area in the household, purchase software that will block access to sexually oriented Web sites, give the password to a 12-step sponsor or friend, and create accountability by "book-ending" his use of the Internet (that is, phone a program friend or sponsor immediately before and after using the computer). Blocking software should also be installed on mobile devices such as iPads or Smartphones.

Before the advent of laptops, iPads, Smartphones, and other mobile devices, when computer access took place either at home or in the workplace, strategies to restore trust involved only the home computer. These are still useful, but no longer enough. Suggest to the addict that he discuss with his partner ways of reassuring her that he is not using his portable electronic device to connect with other partners, view pornography, or engage in other activities that were part of his previous acting out. One way is to purchase and install blocking software that can function not only on your home computer but also on multiple mobile devices. Software websites will inform you if their product is appropriate for your devices. A good resource for comparing various products is www.sexualrecovery.com/online-controls-for-sex-romance-addicts.php. Some software provides accountability; that is, an "accountability partner" is notified if the user attempts to visit websites that are blocked, uses the GPS function on his mobile device, and various other activities. The accountability partner may be the therapist, a Twelve-Step sponsor, or a supportive friend. It is not a good idea to use the addict's partner as his accountability partner, especially early on when the partner is traumatized and reactive. Putting the partner in a parental, monitoring role can adversely affect the couple relationship.

Explain to the addict that these strategies not only reassure the partner, but they also actually protect the addict and help prevent slips. They can be viewed as the equivalent of a recovering alcoholic taking the drug Antabuse (disulfiram). If alcohol is ingested by a person who has this drug in his body, he will experience headache, nausea, vomiting, chest pain, anxiety, and other unpleasant symptoms. Thus, the drug serves as a deterrent to the alcoholic who might otherwise take a drink on impulse.

Most partners want to know why the addict did what he did. Rather than focus on the why, it is more beneficial for the couple to talk about the meaning of the addictive behavior to each of them. How to do a formal disclosure is outlined earlier in the book. Once the anger and fear have subsided, discuss what aspects of the relationship are sources of emotional distress for the partner or addict. Explore with the couple alternative ways of viewing those situations or other ways to interact during those times. Also make plans for dealing with other high-risk times such as work difficulties, financial hardships, accidents, or illnesses. Be certain the couple recognizes that anniversary dates of the disclosure or discovery or other particularly painful events can be difficult occasions. These anniversaries tend to re-ignite the partner's anger and the addict's shame and they need to be planned for appropriately. The couple needs to increase their ability to cope with emotional distress in general and have firm plans for those anniversary dates.

Inability to manage intimacy is often paradoxically seen after a particularly loving or pleasurable time together. Whichever member of the couple is least able to tolerate closeness will re-establish distance through conflict or by ignoring the other. The resulting confusion creates mismanaged fear, which then becomes a trigger for either addictive or codependent acting out. Resuming sexual intimacy also may trigger flashbacks in the partner. Predict the likelihood of these phenomena and co-create strategies with the couple to help them manage.

More intense flashbacks and other post traumatic symptoms in the partner can throw the couple into another crisis. Intrusions by a former affair partner, an anniversary date, the discovery of old acting out paraphernalia, or the exposure of a lie to a partner about an important event can trigger obsessive thoughts for the partner. The addict's best defense is to agree his past behavior was wrong, express sorrow, and then ask if there is anything he can do *now* to remedy the situation. It is the therapist's task in session to help the partner get unstuck. Ask her to identify any additional unanswered questions and to recognize if she is mismanaging an emotional state. Encourage her to express pain without blaming. Advise her to set aside specific times for obsessing, to use a thoughts/feelings journal to help her identify thinking errors, and to develop plans of action. Meditation and prayer are also helpful for most people. Some therapists have found it helpful to use EMDR (eye movement desensitization and reprocessing) to reprocess and extinguish the power of traumatic memories of the betrayal.

It is common for one or both of the parties to have other addictions, depression, or anxiety. Both partners need to address and begin treatment of any other addictive behavior. If severe depression and anxiety are present, consider referral to a psychiatrist for prescription medication. However, remember that some depression and anxiety is normal; it is important for the client to learn to manage those emotional states rather than medicate them away.

If the couple decides to end the marriage, then the goal of therapy is to gain closure and determine what, if any relationship, they want to have with each other. If they share children, help them to negotiate how to manage the responsibilities of co-parenting.

Beginning Repair Work

We have outlined a number of activities for couples to begin the healing process. Encourage the couple to talk about what gives them hope for the future and brainstorm ways in which they can engage in relationship-enhancing behaviors. Most couples can recall some of the early fond memories of their relationship to rekindle these good feelings. Have them talk about how they fell in love in the first place and what attributes attracted each of them to the other. If the couple expresses resistance to this approach, have them focus instead on how they'd like their relationship to be now. Ask them to list the qualities of a best friend and to decide what they want to do differently each day to demonstrate that they are the other's best friend. In Chapter 9 we reviewed several ways to have the addict work toward rebuilding trust. Checklists of how things have improved are very useful.

Most couples have engaged in dysfunctional patterns of attack-defend, pursue-distance, nag-procrastinate, and blame-placate. Children or in-laws are often triangulated into these patterns of interacting that reduce or create homeostasis within the relationship. Couples who learn to relate directly can enhance their time together.

People in recovery often devote so much time and effort on recovery activities that couples forget to go on dates with each other or to spend some alone time together. Encourage them to set aside time to be together to either talk or just to enjoy each other's company. Suggest a homework assignment in which partner and addict alternate in asking for the date, selecting the location, and even driving to and paying for the date.

Encourage open discussion in session of the couple's sexual relationship. As mentioned earlier, this often will provoke flashbacks and difficult times. After a period of hard work, it is particularly useful for the couple to plan a special occasion in which to declare their renewed commitment and trust with each other. Discuss how to optimize sex for both partners. Rather than focus on what behaviors are off-limits, have the partner determine first what affectionate, loving, and sexual behaviors she is open to.

After that time, we recommend that couples schedule "intimacy times." If sex happens, fine. If not, we encourage holding each other, kissing, and other forms of intimacy. These activities can be particularly fulfilling when they are part of the couple's date night.

After couples have been in therapy and recovery for several years, the partner is ready to engage in additional sexual behaviors that both might enjoy, but which may feel more risky to one or the other. Frequently, the addict may hesitate to request a particular sexual act for fear that the partner will think he wants to act out. Encourage couples to dialogue about their sexual desires and to explore whether this is an option. Reading aloud from a recommended book on sexuality (*Erotic Intelligence* by Alex Katehakis is one we recommend) is a great way for couples to discuss whether they would want to participate in a behavior or not. However, if the addict has used the partner as a way to act out, these couples need to first process extensively with each other the meaning of sexual expression.

Special Areas of Concern for Therapists

Below we discuss some special areas of concern for therapists who are counseling sex addicts and their partners.

Therapists Who Have Little or No Experience in Dealing with Sex Addiction

In our research with couples dealing with sexual addiction, the primary complaint was that the therapist was unfamiliar with sex addiction and that the therapist's approach prolonged the addict's denial about the extent of the problem. If you have little or no experience with sex addiction, let the couple know and be willing to address their marital problems with a therapist who is familiar with these issues. Some therapists find it useful to get peer supervision from someone familiar with sex addiction diagnosis and treatment.

High-Risk Acting Out

Sex addicts engage in a variety of behaviors that the partner may or may not view as extramarital—for example, collecting Internet pornography, telephone sex, viewing nude dancers, masturbation with another person on the computer, and sexual massage. Most sex addicts, however, do engage in behaviors that involve sexual contact with another person, often without protection from sexually transmitted diseases. This was evident in the results of our survey, which found that of the 100 sex addict responses, 91 percent reported engaging in sexual behaviors that included another person.

Involvement with another person presents a different threat or cost to the relationship than solitary sexual activities. For one, it increases the risk that the partner will want to leave the relationship, and therefore makes it more difficult for the addict to disclose the behaviors. For another, involvement with another person risks exposure of the addict—and by extension, the partner— to sexually transmitted diseases. The risk of infection with a sexually transmitted disease, especially HIV, presents an ethical dilemma for the therapist who learns about a concealed affair. Given the ethical stipulation that therapists report to authorities when a person's life is in danger, an HIV positive addict might be asked by his or her therapist to disclose to the partner. If the addict has not yet been tested, you will want to suggest he be tested immediately.

Other Areas of Safety

In any informed consent letter or discussion, it is required by most licensure practice acts to declare to the potential client the limitations of confidentiality regarding sexual or physical abuse of a minor or others who do not have the ability to make an informed decision. The duty to report abuse and potential homicide or suicide are generally clear but can be different from state to state. Many therapists question their duty to report users of pornography. Possession of child pornography is a crime in all states but viewing is less clear. Make sure you have checked your licensure practice act and law enforcement about the requirements in your state and inform your clients prior to the first session.

If the addict or the partner fears for their physical safety, appropriate steps should be taken to get the couple to separate for a short period of time. If domestic violence has been part of the couple's history, she needs to have a back-up plan for leaving if the situation increases in volatility. Especially when it is the woman who has acted out sexually outside the marriage, the therapist needs to assess the risk of violence before recommending disclosure.

Another area of safety concerns potential victims of sexual offenders. When sexual behaviors include victimizing others, the therapist's first priority needs to be to get the client to stop the behaviors. A significant therapist mistake is to focus on getting the addict to understand the sources of the behavior, resolve childhood trauma, etc., without directly addressing the behavior itself. For example, in his book *Therapists Who Have Sex with Their Patients*, Dr. Herbert Strean describes his treatment of a male therapist who over time had had sexual relations with several female clients. He relates how over a four-year period, using psychoanalytic psychotherapy, he was finally able to bring the patient to sufficient mental health that he no longer felt compelled to get his emotional needs met through sexual contact with clients. However, the issue of the trauma done to the clients and the need to immediately stop the behavior was reportedly never directly addressed, and the patient apparently continued the behavior for an extended time period while undergoing therapy. (Sexual relations with a therapy client or patient is so potentially damaging to the patient that it is prohibited by professional associations and licensing bodies throughout the United States and Canada, and is a felony in several states.)

Similarly, when a client relates to a helping professional that her partner disclosed to her some potentially victimizing sexual activities, it is a mistake to underestimate the gravity of the situation. For example, in a survey of partners of cybersex addicts, we heard from a young woman that when she was engaged to be married, her fiancé admitted he was downloading pornographic images of underage girls from the computer. She went to her minister for counseling, to discuss her options. She reported that the minister dismissed her concern, stating that her fiancé was probably "just curious," and that after they were married, his curiosity would undoubtedly be satisfied by having sex with his wife. Unfortunately, the husband's behavior continued long past the marriage, and the wife was now worried about his risk of arrest.

The bottom line is, when a client admits to behaviors that are illegal, dangerous, or involve victimizing others, therapists must make it their priority to assure the safety of the addict, spouse, and potential victims. Therapists need to be familiar with the laws of their state regarding reporting to police information the therapist received from a client regarding sexual activity involving underage children, including possession of child pornography. An excellent review was provided by Charles Samenow, in his 2012 article," Child Pornography and the Law: A Clinician's Guide." Additionally, ATSA (www.atsa.org) and SASH (www.sash.net) are two organizations that provide specialized training for the assessment and treatment of sex offenders.

Mismanaged Anger

In the recent past, partners were encouraged to rage through their anger, hitting mock images of the addict or perpetrator. Research has shown that this approach to helping people express their anger is usually not helpful; instead it keeps the person in a state of rage and connected to their trauma rather than released from it. It is more helpful for the partner to identify what she is angry about, note the level of anger on a scale of 0 to 10, and then make a plan for reducing her anger so that she can think clearly about any action that needs to be taken. Sometimes therapists have partners write anger letters and read them aloud, but it is important that the partner is accountable in that letter about how she contributes to the situation or makes the situation worse for herself. Finally, she should declare what would make things better for her today since nothing can be done about the past.

Premature Diagnosis

When a client presents with a sexual problem, ferreting out its cause may require some detective work. An all-too-common therapist mistake is to diagnose without obtaining an adequate sexual history of both the addict and the partner. For example, a client who complains that her husband is not interested in sex with her may indeed be married to someone who has a sexual aversion disorder or sexual dysphoric disorder (also termed sexual anorexia), but alternatively, he may be an active sex addict who is spending hours every night downloading pornography and masturbating, and that is why he is no longer interested in partner sex. If a client describes her own loss of interest in sex with her husband, she may have sexual anorexia, but alternatively she may be reacting appropriately to living with a spouse who has disclosed that he spends hours masturbating on the computer, and who, after ten years of marriage suddenly wants her to participate in unusual sexual practices with which she is uncomfortable. Take the time to ask enough questions to get a full understanding of what is happening in the relationship. When a couple has mismatched sexual interests or activities, do not hasten to diagnose the problem as an uptight, sexually uninformed, or prudish partner. Rather than instinctively blaming the wife, get a thorough history.

In other cases, the diagnosis may be correct, but the labeling may be premature. Partners are very sensitive to being labeled along with the addict. In the past we have used the term coaddict and codependent for the partner of an addict. However, through our own research and that of others and our clinical experience, such labels rarely help the partner begin to see her part in the dance. Partners report that they experience the situation as traumatic and while some of their behavior may have codependent traits, they do not find the label helpful. After the chaos begins to subside, it is easier for the partner to see that some of her behaviors have contributed to the situation with the couple. Early on, let her hear those labels at support group meetings from other partners in similar situations. Introduce the concept, if appropriate, after you (the therapist) understand the context of her situation.

Timing of Disclosure

As we have described earlier, the addict most commonly discloses initially when the partner is about to learn the truth anyway, or when the partner has already learned some incriminating information. Other addicts, however, develop so much guilt that they feel a huge buildup of pressure to unburden. At some point they may dump everything precipitously, without considering the consequences for the spouse. Although addicts often initiate therapy because their partner insists or encourages this after obtaining some information, some addicts begin therapy before their partner knows anything about their addiction. If the addict is in treatment with you, what should you do when your client wants to come clean to his unsuspecting partner, someone who has no therapist herself nor any 12-step support? In our research, we heard from many partners how traumatizing it was for them to have unexpectedly been provided with painful and terrifying information when they had no support for themselves. Although we favor early disclosure for reasons we previously discussed, we recommend that you begin to plan with the addict a joint meeting with the spouse – but hold it only after she has begun to see a therapist herself. The addict can tell her that he's been working in therapy to deal with some serious problems he's had which impact the relationship, that he needs her help, that he would like her to come with him to a session with you, and that for her to have her own therapist would be a big help.

If, as is more usual, the couple comes to see you after the initial disclosure, all you can do is support and validate the partner and process the disclosure with the couple. When there is additional material to disclose, doing so in session with you is likely to be most helpful for the partner. If the addict has written a letter to the partner, process that letter in the session. Discourage the addict from disclosing or giving a letter to the partner outside the session or without you first reading it and making comments or recommendations.

Earlier in this book we discussed the adverse consequences of disclosure by an addict during treatment, at a time when the spouse has no support to deal with the effects on her of the information. If the addict is in treatment elsewhere, if the partner is not able to be with him at the center for the initial or for further divulging, arrange with the treatment center to have him reveal any further information only when she is in session with you.

Use of Outside Monitoring and Polygraph

Some therapists recommend private detectives and polygraph testing to monitor the activities of the addict. While our research has shown that partners who requested a polygraph to verify the addict's report of his or her behavior also report it as helpful to increase trust, polygraph testing needs to be used with a caution. Other than baseline verification in the truth-seeking stage early in recovery, we do not recommend this type of monitoring unless the addict agrees that outside monitoring will help him remain in recovery. A couple's relationship built on this much distrust is doomed to become a reenactment of unresolved parent-child issues. At some point the partner has to mature enough to tolerate her own discomfort of not being able to be sure of anything but herself.

Saving Face

Often the partner will declare: "If you ever do x, y, z I am leaving you." Then time goes by, the addict does well, and trust is re-established to a great degree. They recommit and everything is going well for a length of time. Then he relapses—usually not to the extent of the original acting out—but he relapses nonetheless. Now the partner is faced with her old threat. All the old memories of the original betrayal resurface as well as the pain. But now it is even harder to leave. The partner has worked hard to make changes herself and has seen changes she has liked in the addict. Now what does she do? We often invite the partner to devise some way that the addict can make restitution by taking certain actions. This may be to have HIV testing done for an extended period of time and wear a condom when they re-engage in sexual activity. Sometimes it is some gift or task he takes on.

While this may seem punitive, when the meaning of the "penance" is reframed through the partner's explanation of "this is what it takes for me to save face with myself for not leaving," the addict often views this in a different light.

Even more powerful is letting the partner discover a new perspective about the addict and herself. With this new perspective, she *can* change her mind.

Countertransference

Since about half of married Americans have had an affair at some point during their marriage, it is quite likely that the therapist has either had an affair or has been in a couple relationship in which an affair happened. It is also common for therapists to have experienced an affair within their own family of origin. If you have not resolved those trust issues, then your countertransference will interfere with being objective in your approach with a couple. Seek assistance from your peer supervisor about these issues and if they persist, refer the couple to another therapist.

Personal Sharing

Although many therapists in recovery disclose some information about their history, it is not advisable to share information about your own affair or sexual acting out history with couples. This type of personal information is private and unless you and your spouse (or former spouse) have gone public with this information, you are betraying the confidentiality of your mate. It is not uncommon for clients who have a less than favorable outcome to then spread stories about you. An overly dependent client may believe that she or he is your best friend because you have shared such intimate information. It is okay to share less intimate stories that teach skills or demonstrate techniques for resolving problems, but using case examples or metaphors are more appropriate.

Don't Give Up Too Soon

It takes between two and five years for individuals to really get comfortable and do well with recovery. That may translate into many years of couple therapy as well. Couples who stop therapy in fewer than twelve sessions are more likely to separate, and the healing process is replaced with destructive interactions. Unfortunately, this leads to more stress and to increased risk of relapse for both addicted person and partner. Although most couples do not remain in weekly therapy beyond the first year or so, most who do well return to therapy from time to time for several sessions when additional difficult problems come up.

Be cautious of the couple in which the addict is quickly remorseful and attentive and the partner is swept off her feet into believing all is well. This style of interacting, common in addicted couples, is likely to lead them back to relapse when stress and anxiety return to the relationship. Gently confront the couple in which you see this wishful thinking and unrealistic "flight into health." Explain to them that the path to recovery is lengthy and at times difficult. Encourage the couple to see therapy as a long-term investment in themselves as well as their relationship.

Conclusions

Throughout this book we have emphasized our belief that disclosure is a cornerstone of healing. Most couples who have experienced disclosure agree with this statement, and recommend the process to other recovering couples. We have also pointed out the adverse consequences of revealing secrets. Clearly, there are some ways of doing this that are better than others. Therapists are in a unique position to facilitate this process for clients, to answer for them questions about the timing of disclosure, about how much to reveal, and to whom, about telling children and parents, employers, and TV talk show hosts, about situations when it might be better *not* to disclose, and about the difference between secrecy and privacy. But therapists need to be educated about disclosure, about its benefits and risks for couples, and about how to best facilitate. We hope this chapter has answered some of your questions about this process.

References

Samenow, Charles. Child pornography and the law: A clinician's guide. *Sexual Addiction and Compulsivity* 19:16-29, 2012.

Strean, H. *Therapists Who Have Sex With Their Patients*. New York: Brunner Mazel, 1993.

Appendix 1
Frequently Asked Questions

Q: I just got married to a man who has been a recovering sex addict for three years. He goes to a Twelve-Step meeting and has a sponsor. He has told me the gist of his past behaviors, but not all the details. I want to know everything so that I can be prepared for the worst in the future. He is reluctant to tell me. Am I right in asking?

Even when an addict reveals what he thinks is everything that he ever did, it is quite common for him to later remember other episodes or behaviors. So you can't totally protect yourself from hearing something difficult in the future about his past. It is natural to feel that having all the information can give you more control over what happens to you. Details are not nearly as helpful as knowing the facts, and indeed may be more harmful. When it comes to someone's addiction history, what is most relevant is what the person is doing *now* to stay sober and live a healthy lifestyle. Is he working an active recovery program? Your focus needs to be on looking at how you can make your own life as healthy as possible.

Q: At our first formal disclosure my husband insisted he told me all the big pieces of his acting out but over the next two years he told me some other things. How can I trust him?

There are two issues here. The first is, why is there a discrepancy between what he told you in the past and what he told you recently? The second is, how can you trust him?

There are several possible reasons why your husband might have not told you everything at the first formal disclosure. One is that he may have thought at the time that he was telling you everything, but actually forgot to mention a few items out of many. Or he may have thought they were not important, but later in recovery realized they were. He might also have acted out while under the influence of alcohol or drugs and had no recollection of the event until much later.

If his delayed disclosure was due to one of these reasons, you need to make a distinction between what happened *before* he got into recovery and afterwards. If before, then your best option is to let go of the old stuff, realize there may still be other events you may hear about, and focus on what he's doing for his recovery at present.

The second, and very common reason is that he may have slipped or relapsed after the initial disclosure. In our research, we found that slips and relapses are very common among sex addicts (all addicts actually) so partners need to plan in advance how to deal with them. Naturally this depends on the type of relapse, whether other people were involved, and whether you are at risk of contracting a sexually transmitted disease. If so, you need to deal with that as soon as possible. Once you ascertain that the behavior did not put *you* at harm's way, then ask for information about your mate's recovery program. If he is actively dealing with his slip or relapse with his therapist, support group, and sponsor, then this is the best reassurance you have that he is working to earn your trust. Trust is earned and not just granted. Behavior and a person's consistency over time is the litmus test for trust. As he demonstrates over time his consistency, motivation, and right action, your trust will return.

Nothing is ever 100% certain, so part of the partner's work is to learn to accept some uncertainty. Interestingly, in a recent study we did about how partners deal with disclosure of relapse, we learned that whereas after the initial disclosure many partners of sex addicts take a black-and-white approach and threaten to leave the relationship, after learning of the relapse they have a more nuanced approach – they understand that addiction may involve relapses, they focus on the addict's recovery work and his honesty, and they are more prepared to see this through if their mate is committed to getting healthier and actively working on it. Their trust is connected more with the addict's commitment to recovery and his willingness to disclose a relapse early on than with the fact that a slip or relapse happened.

Q: After three years of "sexual sobriety" from pornography, massage parlors, and prostitutes, my husband had a slip recently – he got on the internet and got involved in some interactive cybersex. He told his sponsor and Twelve-Step group right away, but was afraid

to tell me because after his initial disclosure three years ago, I had asked for a separation. But this time although I'm upset about this, I'm just glad he's actively working on dealing with this slip. Am I in denial? Am I being codependent?

In earlier days, partners who chose to stay with an addict in recovery who relapsed or slipped were quickly labeled codependent and were assumed to be staying with their mate because they weren't healthy enough to leave. But what we now recognize from our research is that partners often choose to stay because they understand the disease and see that their mate is making efforts and that he was honest with them. They perceive his recovery as a "work in progress." These partners are weighing the pros and cons, and making reasoned choices that work for them. If your husband were back into his active addiction, lying to you, and not willing to change, that would be a different story. But from what you are telling us, our answer is no, you are not in denial or codependent. And don't be surprised if you find yourself wanting more information about what strategies he has put in place for avoiding further Internet slips (Internet filters, parental controls, accountability partners, etc.). This is a natural part of wanting to feel safe, not a sign of codependency.

Q: My wife recently began going out two evenings a week, but won't tell me exactly where. She says she's attending some type of self-help meeting to deal with some emotional problems she's been having. I'm getting very nervous about what's going on. I'm afraid there's something big she's not telling me. What should I do?

It sounds as if your wife is hesitant to reveal to you some things that might be painful for you to hear. This situation is usually best handled in a therapy session. Is she seeing a counselor at this point? If so, you might suggest that she talk with her counselor about arranging a meeting for the three of you in which she could tell you what's going on. You certainly deserve to hear this. But don't be surprised if the counselor suggests that you might want to have a counselor for yourself to process whatever you might learn about. If your wife does not already have a counselor, then we think it would be really a good idea for the two of you to find a couples' counselor to see together to talk about this situation.

Q: In the past few months my husband seems to have lost interest in sex with me. Instead of coming to bed at night, he disappears into his den, where he stays for hours on the computer. He gets angry when I ask him questions, and says he's working hard on some projects, but on occasion when I've walked in on him, he acts very defensive and quickly turns off the computer. I suspect he is involved in cybersex. How can we deal with our marriage problems if he won't tell me what's going on?

You cannot solve your marital problems alone; even if he doesn't have an addiction problem, your relationship is being affected by the computer use. Try talking to your mate when he is not at the computer, first stating that you miss your relationship with him and would like to get into couple's counseling to see if there is something you can do to improve things. You may also take the direct approach: Tell him you are fearful for him and your marriage, that you have heard about Internet and cybersex addiction, and are scared that that may be happening to him. Suggest that you both see a counselor familiar with this to determine if there is a problem. Unfortunately, unless he is seriously worried about his use, he will most likely refuse.

As long as you continue trying to convince your husband that his behavior is a problem for both of you while he resists, you are still in the one-down position. You need to start taking care of yourself by determining if you want to be in a relationship that is consumed with computer use behind closed doors. If not, you may have to play hard ball for him to understand that you are serious – tell him that unless he seeks help with you or unless he starts using the computer in front of you and is willing to show you what he does, then you are leaving. However, DO NOT threaten to leave unless you are willing and able to follow through

Q: My husband and I have been married 20 years. Ten years ago, when I was feeling strongly the lack of intimacy between us, I got involved in a brief affair with a coworker. After a month, I realized it wasn't the answer to my problems, and I broke it off. My husband has been recovery for a year from his sex addiction and I have been in recovery for my codependent traits. He has disclosed all of his acting-out behaviors to me. Should I tell him about this affair?

What's good for the goose is also good for the gander. If you expected him to be honest with you about his sexual acting out, then does he not also expect you to be honest about yours? If you are both in recovery, then we assume that you practice a program of rigorous honesty. Your husband might be angry and hurt when he hears about your brief affair, but the two of you will get past it. In our research, we learned that men who are themselves in recovery, especially from sex addiction, tend to be much more understanding and forgiving about a wife's affair than are other men, especially when this happened ten years ago.

Q: I saw my good buddy's wife sitting in a coffee shop with another guy. They were holding hands, and occasionally they kissed. My buddy thinks he has a great marriage. Should I tell him what I saw?

Would you want to find out from your buddy or your wife if the situation were reversed? Most people would want to hear this from their mate. Have a chat with his wife. Tell her what you saw and that you think it is her responsibility to be honest with him about the trouble in their marriage. Tell her you hope they can get help and work things out but you won't keep the secret for her. Let her know you realize that figuring out how and when to tell him isn't easy, but you will tell him in another week unless she does. Remind her that you remain a support for both of them should he or she need someone to talk to after the disclosure.

Q: When I was 15, I got pregnant and gave up the child for adoption. I've felt a lot of shame over the years about my early sexual behavior, and never told my husband. My daughter is now 21, and I'd very much like to try to find her. Should I tell my husband? I think my husband would forgive me for my behavior, but I also think he'd be very angry about my keeping this from him all these years. I hesitate to rock the boat when we have a very good marriage.

A big secret in a marriage or committed relationship constitutes a barrier to intimacy and emotional connection. This secret may be decades old, but it obviously is an important part of your current inner landscape. That's why you need to tell him, especially since you have a very good marriage. Yes, he may be angry or, more likely, disappointed that you didn't trust him enough in the past to share this secret with him but if he gets to hear about your shame and fear as a teen, it seems probable that he will soon be by your side in this goal.

A friend of mine, who knew she'd been adopted at birth, began searching for her birth mother after her adoptive mother died when my friend was 40 years old. She soon found her and wrote her a letter, giving her own date of birth and hospital where she was born, but otherwise couched in sufficiently vague language that if the older woman had not told anyone, the letter wouldn't give her away. Her biological mother replied, but said she hadn't told her husband or children of her teenage pregnancy, so she hesitated to meet my friend. Shortly thereafter the woman disclosed to her husband. His reaction was to strongly encourage his wife to invite my friend to visit. As a result, my friend met her birth mother and her four biological sisters, whom she strongly resembles. She now has a whole new family, and her birth mother was able finally, at age 58, to let go of the shame she had felt all these years.

Q: My parents don't know about my husband's sex addiction or his recovery program. As for my own recovery, I told them I'm going to a "women's support group," which they think is just an opportunity for women to complain about their husbands. I'd like to be able to tell them more, but my husband is sure they'd be very judgmental and negative about him, and he's probably right. Should I keep them in the dark?

What to tell your parents is something that you and your husband can decide. If your parents have been judgmental in the past, you might want to talk with them generally about working on your relationship while getting support for yourself.

Q: What's the best way to tell our fifteen-year old daughter and seventeen-year-old son about my husband's sex addiction? He's been sober for three years and I go to S-Anon.

A friend of mine who was divorcing her husband told her teenage daughter, with great trepidation, that her husband had had multiple affairs. Her daughter's reaction was, "Oh, Mom, for years you were the only one in the neighborhood who didn't know about this. I was so angry with you for being such a doormat and ignoring what was going on right under your nose. I'm glad you finally found out and are doing something about it!" My friend was shocked and relieved.

Children often know more than you think, but they take their cues from their parents. If you and your husband have said nothing to them, they are likely to say nothing to you. It's better to have things out in the open. Your children are old enough to know both about addiction and sexuality and are at the age in which kids are talking about both and experimenting lots. Ask them for a block of uninterrupted time for a serious talk. Both you and your husband should be present. Tell them that you want to share information that is hard for you to talk about and you realize they may not want to hear. (Most kids do not want to have this sensitive information. At the same time, they want some explanation about various things that have happened connected to your behaviors.) Because there may be a genetic link to addiction, and because most addictive behavior begins in adolescence, they need to know so that they can be aware of the warning signs of any addiction. Remind them that people can become addicted to behaviors as well as substances. Disclose that he is a recovering addict and that his drug of choice has been sex. Tell them that Dad has been honest with you about what he did in his sex addiction. Often in first conversations, specific information is omitted, especially with younger children. However, if you and your husband agree on the content, you may give teenagers more information, leaving out specific details. For example, he can say

"I got involved with viewing pornography and compulsive masturbation. While masturbation is healthy for some people, for me, it was a way I used to escape and to avoid feeling anything."

Here is a chance for him to talk about the values that guide his recovery. "I also want to say that I now feel strongly that most of the time pornography objectifies women and does not provide any real opportunity for learning how to be with other people much less solve problems. I feel bad about how I used it. It took me away from Mom and caused problems in our relationship."

You might chime in here about your codependent traits if you have them. It may be useful to say that experimental use of certain 'adult' behaviors or drugs to alter your mood is common among young people, but kids who have addiction in their background need to be careful not to fall into the trap of believing this is a solution to their problems.

Now ask if they have any questions or want to say anything. Be quiet and give them a chance to get beyond the discomfort of speaking about this. To end, tell them if they ever have any questions to let you or their Dad know. Tell them that you love them. Do take opportunities to bring this up again so it becomes easier for everyone to talk about.

Q: The other day I caught my twelve-year-old son looking at Internet pornography on his own computer. He doesn't know about my husband's problem with cybersex addiction, and I was horrified to think that he's already involved in the same behavior that almost made me leave his father. I know that kids, especially boys, are very curious about sex, so hopefully this is just normal behavior for his age. I don't want to make a mountain out of a molehill. How do I talk to him about this without making it so forbidden that it becomes all the more desirable for him?

Think about your values. What do you want your son to know about treating women with dignity rather than making them an object? What would you say if your twelve-year old was experimenting with alcohol? Many men in recovery speak to their adolescent sons about this issue. First they explain how people can be addicted to both drugs as well as behavior; some then disclose their own addiction. (At some point you need to discuss your addiction because your children have your genes, thus increasing their propensity towards addiction.) Second, they acknowledge that it is normal to be curious about women's bodies and sex, but that pornography is not the best way to learn. Then they give the adolescent a few age-appropriate sexuality books or together look up more appropriate sex education cites on the computer such as those listed on www.SIECUS.org. . Additionally, they remind the young men that the woman in the picture is someone's sister or daughter and ask if they would want someone looking at and having sexual thoughts or masturbating to images of their sister or daughter. This leaves the door open to further discussions of healthy masturbation, sex within a committed relationship, or any other issues that may come up.

Even if your husband does not reveal his addiction, it is important for him to tell your son that although he viewed in his life, he is no longer going to do it because it interferes with his relationship with you and because it shows disrespect to women. Oh yes, be sure to tell him that you do not want him to view pornography on the computer, his cell phone or elsewhere in your home.

Q. Our children are young – four, six, and ten. Should we tell them about my wife's addiction? We are both seeing a therapist and attending Twelve-Step meetings.

It's never too early to provide your children with information, as long as it's done in an age-appropriate ways. Young children can be told, "Mommy and Daddy have been having some difficulties so we are going to a counselor to help us. It has nothing to do with you. We are not planning to split up."

Q: I am in a same-sex relationship. My spouse recently recognized that he is a sex addict and now attends a Twelve-Step meeting. He suggested I attend a local S-Anon meeting in our city. I've heard that most of the people at those meetings are women. Will they accept a gay man?

S-Anon is a program of recovery for those who have been affected by someone else's sexual behavior. S-Anon is based on the Twelve Steps and the Twelve Traditions of Alcoholics Anonymous. Their material says, "The primary purpose of S-Anon is to recover from the effects upon us of another person's sexaholism, and to help families and friends of sexaholics." Your religion or sexual orientation is immaterial. As you've heard, men are definitely in the minority at meetings of S-Anon (and COSA, another Twelve-Step program for families and friends), but what you all share is a common experience of having been affected by someone else's sex addiction. You will surely be welcomed, and it will not take you long to realize you are among friends.

Q: My husband is the one with the sex addiction. He's the one who needs fixing. I'm the one who was lied to and betrayed. So why am I being told that I should see a therapist and go to self-help meetings?

You're right – your husband is the one with the addiction problem. However, as a result, you are now experiencing distress. It's evident from your question that you have strong feelings about what has happened to you. Being lied to (often repeatedly) and betrayed is a traumatic experience. Partners feel anger, shock, depression, distrust, uncertainty about what to do now, shame, and often physical symptoms such as fatigue, insomnia, and inability to concentrate. A knowledgeable therapist can support you and validate your feelings, and help you figure out what your options are. As for Twelve-Step self-help meetings such as S-Anon and COSA, there you will find other people who've had experiences similar to yours, and who *really understand*. They have walked the path you are treading now, and can share their "experience, strength, and hope." The Twelve-Step program is a series of steps that helps you recover from your experience and be able to reclaim the positive things in your life.

Q: I'm so angry with my husband, but he doesn't seem to get it. He hasn't asked for my forgiveness. Can I forgive him nonetheless?

Forgiveness means being able to remember the past without reliving the pain. It means no longer giving some who has hurt you "free rent in your head," but rather letting go of the resentment, pain, and other negative emotions you feel toward that person. That's why you keep hearing that forgiveness is for *you*, not for the person who hurt you.

The key is, there are several kinds of forgiveness. Many people are quick to say "I forgive you," when in fact nothing has changed in their head. This is a superficial, meaningless gesture, which Janis Abrahms Spring calls "cheap forgiveness." Genuine forgiveness, in contrast, is something someone else *earns* not only by apologizing and asking for it, but also by making amends and by changing their behavior in a sincere effort to remove the source of your pain. If your husband "doesn't get it" and won't engage in the healing process, then genuine forgiveness is not currently an option for you. However, there is another healthy alternative for you, which Spring calls "acceptance" This consists of taking care of yourself and getting the help you need to be able to let go of your anger and pain and figure out what kind of relationship you can have with him that will not be unhealthy for you, while recognizing that he may never change. This may mean staying in the marriage while getting other support, or leaving, depending on your circumstances and your goal.

Q. My spouse came out as gay. Now what do I do?

Take your time in making decisions and take care of yourself. If you don't have one, get a therapist. Even though you may be afraid to tell anyone else, having someone to talk to is important. Share with a trusted friend or family member. Finding support on the Internet (www.straightspouse.org) is another great way to start. Expect to have a full array of emotions and feel what you are feeling at the moment. This is obviously a huge loss, even though you won't be living a lie anymore. Be ready to grieve the loss of what you thought you had. After some time, decide what is important to you, honor the values that guide you, and then take steps that reflect a healthy future. You and your spouse have a lot of decisions ahead, including the future of your marriage.

Q. My spouse says he has had sex with other men. Is he gay?

Not necessarily. Sometimes straight men have sex with men despite having a heterosexual identity. For them it isn't necessarily about romance or sexual attraction; in some cases it is about sexual arousal and just being able to have sex with someone who is accessible. Some straight men are addicted and seek someone who is less available, because they need to take more risk in order to obtain the same "high". Some men are curious and want to experiment; others have a history of sexual abuse and they are reenacting some part of the abuse in an effort to figure it out. Others are not sure if they are gay but act on their attraction to other men. And some men are gay and have kept this secret for a host of reasons.

Q. I'm a gay man in a long-term committed relationship. Long ago we agreed to be monogamous, which is what I've always wanted. But on multiple occasions I've learned that my partner John has in fact had sex with other men. When I've confronted him and told him how much this hurts me and that it feels like a betrayal, he says that it means nothing, it's just part of being gay, and has nothing to do with our relationship. He doesn't think it's a problem and obviously isn't willing to change. What should I do?

Couples in a committed relationship, whether gay or straight, often have different preferences regarding sexual activities. These preferences may involve particular sexual activities, and even the freedom to have sex with other people. In order for the relationship to work, the couple needs to come to some compromise about what is acceptable in the relationship and what isn't. Some things are negotiable between two people, and others are not, and the couple needs to agree on this. They also need to agree not to lie to each as a means of getting around any agreement. If you and your partner can't come to terms on this, then it would be advisable for the two of you to see a counselor together in order to work this out. It's possible that John has a problem with sex addiction, so the counselor will need to be familiar with this disorder. In any case, if your partner is unwilling to go to counseling with you, then you may need to decide whether you want to stay in the relationship.

Appendix 2
Recovery Resources

I. Twelve-Step Resources

These mutual-help programs have meetings in many locations throughout the U.S. and some other countries. They also have online reading material, information about location of meetings, and some have online meetings.

Twelve-Step programs for Sex Addicts

Sexaholics Anonymous
e-mail: saico@sa.org
www.sa.org
Tel: (615) 370-6062

Sex & Love Addicts Anonymous
www.slaafws.org
(210) 828-7900

Sex Addicts Anonymous
e-mail: info@saa-recovery.org
web: www.sexaa.org/
(800) 477-8191
(713) 869-4902

Sexual Compulsives Anonymous (SCA)
web: www.sca-recovery.org
Tel: (800) 977-HEAL

Sexual Recovery Anonymous (SRA)
email: info@sexualrecovery.org
www.sexualrecovery.org

For the Partner or Family Member:

Codependents of Sex Addicts (COSA)
email: info@cosa-recovery.org
www.cosa-recovery.org
866) 899-COSA (2672)

S-Anon International Family Groups
email: sanon@sanon.org
www.sanon.org
(615)833-3152
800) 210-8141

For teenage family members of sexual addicts:

S-Ateen
Contact: S-Anon International Family Groups

For Couples

Recovering Couples Anonymous (RCA)
email: wso-rca@recovering-couples.org
website: www.recovering-couples.org
877-663-2317
(781) 794-1456

For Sexual Trauma Survivors:

Survivors of Incest Anonymous (SIA)
website: siawso.org
(410) 893-3322

Incest Survivors Anonymous (ISA)
website: lafn.org
Tel: (562) 428-5599

For Sex Workers:

Sex Workers Anonymous
(702) 612-1253

II. Other Resources

Society for the Advancement of Sexual Health (SASH)
email: SASH@SASH.net
website: www.sash.net
(770) 541-9912

The Society for the Advancement of Sexual Health (SASH) is a nonprofit multidisciplinary organization dedicated to scholarship, training, and resources for promoting sexual health and overcoming problematic sexual behaviors (sex addiction, hypersexual disorder, out of control sexual behavior, sexual impulsivity, sexual abuse.) The website contains educational material including position papers, contact information for Twelve-step programs, and a list of relevant books, as well as contact information for knowledgeable sex addiction therapists all over the U.S and internationally. SASH sponsors an academic journal, *Sexual Addiction and Compulsivity: The Journal of Treatment and Prevention*, and also an annual conference.

Straight Spouse Network
www.ssnetwk.org

Index

Addicts
    accountability, need for 155, 168
    core beliefs 98-99
    "damage control" 69
    denial by 28
    dysfunctional family of origin 17
    effect of the addiction on children 84-89
    emotions during disclosure 52
    fear of partner leaving 66, 94
    low self-esteem 19
    need to demonstrate changed behaviors 28, 116, 153
    need to demostrate remorse 75, 77, 178
    negative consequences of disclosure for 61-63, 160
    obsessive thinking
    positive consequences of disclosure for 11, 53-56, 160
    relapse 160, 167
    shame 52, 67, 83, 84, 168
    values 165, 187
Amedure, Scott 34
Betrayal 11, 12, 50, 57, 59, 118, 166, 177
Boundaries 84, 102, 143, 164
Brown, Emily 12
Burton-Nelson, Mariah 28, 75
Buxton, Amity Pierce 124
Children
    boundaries 21, 88
    development 9, 21, 17
    disclosure to 83-109
    effect of discovering parent acting out 111-113
    effect of parental addiction on 83-89, 128
    good parenting of 98-108
    if addict is unwilling to disclose to 95, 106
    reactions to disclosure 90-93
    reasons to disclose to 90-93
    sexual abuse of 87-89
    united front by parents 107
    what children don't want to know 97
    what children want to know 95-98
    why children lie 15, 35
Clementi, Tyler 35
Clinton, Pres. Bill 7, 37
Computer strategies 167-168
Codependency 10, 84
Couple relationship
    agreement on future disclosures 114
    balancing individual & couple recovery 170
    ending the relationship 156, 169
    healing/repairing 12, 27, 41, 67, 77, 81, 116, 156, 170
    rebuilding trust 67, 153-156
    relapse, effect on 12,
    secrets, lies, dishonesty- effect on 11
    separation 64-65, 67, 108, 142
    threats to leave 64-65, 67, 114, 166

Disclosure
- after an arrest 37, 136-137
- attempts at damage control 38
- by phone, text, email, or letter 31, 33, 34
- consequences of 49-68, 74
- delayed disclosure – reasons for 41-42
- discovery of parent's acting out 112-113
- domestic violence, risk of 38, 173
- during addict's inpatient addiction treatment 77-78
- effects on addict 25, 36,
- effects on partner 16, 25, 37, 39, 64, 67, 70
- effects on relationship 24, 26
- how much to reveal 35-37, 42-43, 182
- how to do it right 69-81
- if addict is unwilling to disclose 95
- inappropriate 30-35, 69, 92, 175
- interim disclosure 44-45
- is a process 39, 41, 167
- letter to partner, child, parent 72-75, 79, 95, 129-131
- meaning of 5, 55, 71
- multiple disclosures 38
- other disclosures 111-126
- negative outcomes 71
- of gay or bisexual identity 123-124
- of long-ago secrets 119-120
- of relapse 42, 66, 81, 114-117
- of sex offending 91, 138-140
- on TV 34-35
- partial disclosure 40-41, 44-45
- partner's decision to stay or leave 26, 63-66
- partner's preparations to hear 78-80
- positive outcomes 5-14, 24, 28, 53-56
- public disclosure 40, 86
- reactions of children 90-93
- reactions of friends 60
- remorse by addict 75
- role of therapist 77
- staggered 37-42, 113, 114, 181-182
- to adolescents 186-189
- to children 77, 83-109, 189
- to friends 135-136
- to new romantic partner 132-5
- to parents or other family members 127, 186
- what children want to know 95-98
- when to disclose 29-35, 80, 185-186
- when not to disclose 6, 12, 117, 140
- why addicts disclose 6-7
- why partners leave 66
- why partners need disclosure 5, 7-10

Earle, Ralph & Marcus 83
Emotions, managing 52-53, 84, 103, 145, 165, 169, 174
Ford, Charles 15
Fossum, Merle 88
Forward, Susan 21
Forgiveness 26-29, 74-75, 190
- acceptance 28
- "cheap forgiveness" 28
- definition 29
- "genuine forgiveness" 29
- refusal to forgive 28
- role in healing 24

Glass, Shirley 61
Goleman, Daniel 102

INDEX

Gottman, John 11, 75, 143, 155
Haffner, Debra 96
Herman, Judith 74
HIV and AIDS 118, 174
Homosexuality 56, 94, 123-124, 189, 191-2
Hope Floats (movie) 35
Honesty 8-9, 11-13, 155
Infidelity 11
Intimacy 6, 11
Jones, Jenny TV Show 34
Jung, Carl 83
Katehakis, Alex 171
Laaser, Mark 101
Lies/dishonesty 11, 15-24
    effects on the partner 8
    effects on the relationship 11, 15-24
    lies partners tell themselves 21-24
    role in development 15-16
    why people lie 15-24
Mason, Marilyn 88
Means, Marsha 142
Newberry, Tommy 157
Nixon, Pres. Richard 7
Partner
    addictions in 60, 78, 169
    boundaries 29, 79, 143
    childhood trauma 17, 65
    codependency 10, 175, 182-3
    core beliefs 99
    denial by 28
    disclosure of addict's relapse 114-117
    disclosure of partner's acting out 184-185
    do they leave after disclosure or discovery? 26, 38, 63-66, 65, 67
    dysfunctional family of origin 9, 17, 65
    eating disorder in 18, 20
    emotions during disclosure 52-53
    family week in mate's addiction treatment 77-78
    fear of abandonment 57, 65
    lies they tell themselves 21-24
    low self-esteem 17-20, 59
    need for recovery program/therapy 117, 189-190
    need for validation 12, 164
    need to know 36, 41, 78, 168, 183, 184
    negative consequences of disclosure for 27, 36, 56-61, 64, 67, 71, 164
    obsessive thinking 36, 57, 84, 166
    personal healing 144-153
    positive consequences of disclosure for 36, 53-56
    post-traumatic stress disorder (PTSD) 8-10,
    preparing to hear a disclosure 78-80
    reactions to disclosure of relapse 66, 116, 177, 183
    risk of HIV and other STDs 31, 50, 59
    relational trauma 8-10, 56-57, 78-79, 175
    setting boundaries 131-32
    sexual trauma victim 130-132
    self-blame 23, 63-64, 125
    threats to leave 64-65, 114
    trusting their own judgment 17
    want to fix the addict 23
    want to know everything 78-79
    why partners lie 21-24

Pittman, Frank 11
Polygraph use 176
Post-traumatic stress disorder (PTSD) 9, 169
Private information vs. Secrets 43, 106
Ravi, Dharun 35
Secrets 15-24,
   the elephant in the living room 20-21, 25
   effects on children 83
   types of 17
   versus private information 43
   when not to tell
Schmitz, Jonathan 34
Schwartzenegger, Gov. Arnold 37
Sex offenders/sex offender registry
   disclosure to children 91
   disclosure to neighbors 137-140
Siegel, Daniel 103
Society for the Advancement of Sexual Health (SASH) 142, 195
Spring, Janis Abrahms 28-9

Steffens, Barbara 142
Strean, Herbert 173
Therapists, guidance for 159-179
   and secret-keeping 44-46, 125
   countertransference 177
   high-risk behavior by client 171-2
   premature diagnosis 174-175
   personal sharing 177-78
   polygraph use 176
   role in disclosure 32, 77
   support for partner 50, 71, 142, 164, 177, 189-190
   timing of disclosure 175-176
Tomm, Karl 27
Trauma for partner 57, 79
Twelve-step programs 49, 62, 65, 71, 115, 147, 163, 165, 167, 181, 189, 193-194
   'Big Book' of AA 49
   role of honesty
Trust, rebuilding 153-155
Weiner, Rep. Anthony 8

Printed in Great Britain
by Amazon.co.uk, Ltd.,
Marston Gate.